Understanding Religious Fundamentalists

This book introduces the prominent role that fundamentalists play in religious, cultural, and political arenas.

It begins by investigating religious fundamentalist groups and their psychological motivations for this counter-cultural adherence. Their extremely varied actions, argues the author, are based on two fundamental beliefs: that God speaks to them personally through his Word; and that they are involved in a cosmic war between God and Satan. Subsequent chapters explore how fundamentalisms meet universal psychological needs for meaning, identity, agency, and self-esteem. Moving from individual psychology to social context, the latter half of the book explores how fundamentalist movements derive and exercise their authority and how leaders may strategise to appeal to external societies. The closing chapters seek to place the growth of fundamentalisms and their continued popularity in the social context of modernity and populism.

With engaging discussion questions and suggestions for further reading, this book is ideal for students of social science and religion, as well as readers interested in the psychological roots of fundamentalism.

Peter Herriot has been an academic and consultant throughout his working life. Most of his work has been in the field of organizational psychology. Since retirement, he has concentrated on the application of social scientific theory and research to the issue of religious fundamentalism. He was brought up in a fundamentalist family.

Routledge Focus on Religion

Theology and Climate Change
Paul Tyson

Religion and Euroscepticism in Brexit Britain
Ekaterina Kolpinskaya and Stuart Fox

Owning the Secular
Religious Symbols, Culture Wars, Western Fragility
Matt Sheedy

Cross-Cultural and Religious Critiques of Informed Consent
Edited by Joseph Tham, Alberto García Gómez, and Mirko Daniel Garasic

Worldview Religious Studies
Douglas J Davies

White Evangelicals and Right-Wing Populism: How Did We Get Here?
Marcia Pally

Rape Culture in the House of David: A Company of Men
Barbara Thiede

Counseling Survivors of Religious Abuse
Paula J. Swindle, Craig C. Cashwell, and Jodi L. Tangen

Understanding Religious Fundamentalists: An Introduction
Peter Herriot

For more information about this series, please visit: www.routledge.com/Routledge-Focus-on-Religion/book-series/RFR

Understanding Religious Fundamentalists
An Introduction

Peter Herriot

LONDON AND NEW YORK

First published 2024
by Routledge
4 Park Square, Milton Park, Abingdon, Oxon OX14 4RN

and by Routledge
605 Third Avenue, New York, NY 10158

Routledge is an imprint of the Taylor & Francis Group, an informa business

© 2024 Peter Herriot

The right of Peter Herriot to be identified as author of this work has been asserted in accordance with sections 77 and 78 of the Copyright, Designs and Patents Act 1988.

All rights reserved. No part of this book may be reprinted or reproduced or utilised in any form or by any electronic, mechanical, or other means, now known or hereafter invented, including photocopying and recording, or in any information storage or retrieval system, without permission in writing from the publishers.

Trademark notice: Product or corporate names may be trademarks or registered trademarks, and are used only for identification and explanation without intent to infringe.

British Library Cataloguing-in-Publication Data
A catalogue record for this book is available from the British Library

ISBN: 978-1-032-75013-2 (hbk)
ISBN: 978-1-032-75014-9 (pbk)
ISBN: 978-1-003-47198-1 (ebk)

DOI: 10.4324/9781003471981

Typeset in Sabon LT Pro
by KnowledgeWorks Global Ltd.

Contents

Introduction	1
PART I **Two Fundamentalisms**	7
1 Brethren and Taliban	9
2 The Brethren: Authority and Separation	15
3 The Taliban: Sharia and Jihad	22
PART II **Fundamentalist Beliefs**	29
4 God's Word	31
5 Cosmic War	38
6 Belief Systems	46
PART III **Motivational Foundations**	53
7 Meaning	55
8 Agency	62
9 Self-esteem	68

PART IV
Social Foundations   75

10   Leadership   77

11   Conformity   83

12   Organisation   89

PART V
Perspectives: Past, Present, and Future   97

13   Modernity   99

14   Populism   106

15   Apocalypse   112

Index   *118*

Introduction

Who are fundamentalists?

Fundamentalists refuse to go away. Having seized the world's horrified attention on 9/11/2001, they have continued to play a prominent role in religious, political, and cultural arenas ever since. Theocratic regimes continue to gain and hold power, for example, in Iran and Afghanistan. And all the while, less newsworthy fundamentalists exercise political pressure in favour of their moral agenda, successfully seek to add to their number by proselytising or procreation, or try to develop alternative and separate communities away from this wicked world. Clearly, there is still an urgent need for a better understanding of fundamentalism and fundamentalists.

This book is intended as an introduction in two senses. It is not a work of original scholarship, but rather a text written for entering students of social science and religion, both those in higher education and interested citizens. And it is also an attempt to introduce readers to fundamentalists as people by examining what they say and do. It starts with the people themselves and only moves on later to discuss their social and political context. This basically psychological approach aims to avoid the frequent dismissal of fundamentalists' beliefs as pre-modern ignorance, and their activities as escapism or terrorism. Rather, we should examine their beliefs very seriously, as they inform, motivate, and justify their actions. I bring to the task an academic career in psychology and a fundamentalist upbringing.

So what is fundamentalism, and who are fundamentalists? *Historians* (1) have traced the use of the term back to its origins in a theological dispute among American Protestants in the early 20th century. They have followed its subsequent development in religion, academia, and American politics in the late 20th century, and then its explosion into the global lexicon after the assault on the United States in 2001. They note that it has by now become a general term of abuse, used by "progressives" about "traditionalists". Which use of the term, then, if any, is it appropriate to employ today?

DOI: 10.4324/9781003471981-1

2 Introduction

In response to the demand for a definition, *sociologists* raise contextual issues (2). What, they ask, is the appropriate level of analysis from which to approach fundamentalism? Is it basically a religious phenomenon, or should it be viewed within the broad social and historical context of modernity and post-modernity? What are its roots in social and political change, and how has it in turn influenced social systems? Further, some worry, is it ethical to impose a categorical label on people to which they themselves might well object?

In this book, I will take a pragmatic position on these questions of definition. For decades, many different social institutions have used the term fundamentalism without disagreeing in a basic way about what it refers to. Government, media, social science, religion, non-governmental organisations, and the arts have all referred to a category of religious movements as fundamentalism. They have not disagreed irreconcilably about which movements fall into this category and have been happy to refer to their adherents as fundamentalists, together with a variety of often pejorative other labels.

Instead, then, of devoting time and effort to formulating a definition, it seems preferable to allow those labelled "fundamentalists" by others to speak for themselves. If we pay careful attention to what they say, we may be able to infer what they believe, what they value, and why they act as they do. Already, however, I have imposed a distinction of my own by differentiating what they *say* from what they *do*. This distinction is, of course, part of our everyday use of language; we frequently refer to people's regular failure to match deeds to words, or, for that matter, words to deeds. Yet we are always doing things by speaking; for example, we can be promising, describing, requesting, accusing, persuading, accusing, and joking. And conversely, when we do things, we are frequently sending messages; our actions are frequently performative in their intent. It is a cliché that the assault of 9/11 was intended to send a message to the world. It is also now a fact of life that live images can be communicated instantly and globally to powerful effect.

So how might we best access the way in which fundamentalists demonstrate to us and to each other what they believe and value? And anyway, how can we possibly hope to draw any worthwhile conclusions from a disparate range of religious movements based on different cultures and acting out a gamut of different narratives? Some fundamentalists do their utmost to avoid any involvement with the world; others engage with it in an attempt to change it, while yet others assault its institutions furiously. Some have developed from within our own historical and cultural perspective, while others are alien to our personal experience.

Structure of this book

It would be impossible to review adequately what is by now known about fundamentalist movements. Accounts have been provided by intrepid media professionals and concerned religious commentators, as well as by academic researchers from a variety of disciplines. This book therefore starts with accounts of just two fundamentalist movements, supported by illustrative reference to others. These movements are chosen from two of the three "religions of the book" (Judaism, Christianity, and Islam). They are the Protestant *Plymouth Brethren* and the Islamist *Taliban*. The Brethren seek primarily to separate themselves from this evil world; the Taliban want to impose sharia law by force upon it. These case studies seek to pay careful attention to various cultural artefacts or elements of these movements, so as to infer beliefs and values. They occupy **Part 1** of the book, and hopefully enable readers to get closer to the mindset of each set of adherents. How, you may ask, can two such utterly different movements be placed in the same religious category? By describing the quiet and peaceful Brethren immediately before the violently aggressive Taliban, I am trying to point up the essential feature of fundamentalism which these polar opposites share in common – two basic beliefs. What I am certainly not doing is implying that Christianity is a more peaceful religion than Islam in general. Religions have the potential to give rise to fundamentalist movements, the large majority of which are not violent. To repeat, not many fundamentalisms are violent, and no religion can be considered more violent than any other.

Part 2 proposes that these two *core beliefs* inform and generate the complex belief and value systems of all fundamentalist movements. They are, first, that the Almighty God speaks to them directly through their holy book and prophets, telling them all they need to know about what to believe and how to act. And second, they are engaged on God's behalf in a cosmic war between God and Satan, good and evil. These core beliefs give rise logically and systematically to a varied set of implications, which, taken together, constitute a coherent and inspirational narrative. First, they generate a wide range of secondary beliefs about the nature of reality, cause and effect, the social world and individuals' position in it, and so on. From these beliefs, fundamentalists derive values such as purity, authority, and obedience, for example, and deplore the values espoused by such movements as secularism, modernity, and feminism. And from these beliefs and values, they there logically follows a range of distinctive norms of behaviour to which they are expected to conform.

Why are fundamentalists so single-mindedly devoted to their movements, and to the beliefs, values, and norms of behaviour which they mandate? What psychological motivation could there possibly be for such counter-cultural adherence? It is not usually because adherents are already authoritarian or damaged people who are attracted to these movements. It is rather, as I argue in **Part 3**, because fundamentalisms are very effective at meeting certain *universal psychological needs*: for example, needs for meaning, identity, agency, and self-esteem. Fundamentalisms provide a simple binary worldview to reduce the uncertainty of the rapidly changing environment. They firmly place their adherents in a prominent position within this worldview, giving them a membership which shapes their view of themselves. Since this position is a highly favourable one, their self-esteem is boosted, for they are valued by God and their fellow adherents. And they feel that, with God on their side, they have a power which enables them to overcome their evil enemy.

In **Part 4**, we start moving from individual psychology to the social context, starting with the immediate context of *the fundamentalist movement* itself. How does a movement derive its authority and exercise it, we may ask. How does it ensure conformity to its beliefs, values, and norms of behaviour? What forms of organisation does it develop to help it achieve these internal sources of power, and also to relate externally to the rest of society? And what roles does leadership play? Are leaders simply particularly pious fundamentalist believers, who ensure that historic and absolute truths based on a past golden age continue to hold sway? Or are they more strategic in their approach, trying to persuade their movement to adapt to changes in its environment and so maintain its appeal and relevance?

Finally, in **Part 5**, I take a broader and more sociologically based perspective, seeking to place the growth of fundamentalisms and their continued popularity in a broad *social context*. I start with a general account of their relationship with the process of modernisation, a topic which has dominated sociological explanations of fundamentalism hitherto. In this account, fundamentalism is explained as a reaction against secularisation and modernity. Their reactionary posture profoundly affects fundamentalisms' relationship with nation states and with other social institutions. This emphasis, however, fails to address recent developments. I argue that many of the key social systems of modernity are currently failing to meet the needs of large sections of global society. As a result, the reaction is not now so much against modernity as such, but rather against its failures to fulfil its prospectus. It manifests itself in the current global growth of populist nationalism. As for the future, fundamentalists' preoccupation with an inevitable apocalypse is now shared by large numbers of secular citizens – a potentially powerful congruence.

The order of these five parts is a deliberate reversal of most accounts of fundamentalism. These typically start with a consideration of its historical, political, and cultural context, emphasising rightly that the roots of social movements, including religious ones, are to be found in their social contexts. However, it seems important from a psychological perspective to start with fundamentalists themselves rather than with their context. I am not proposing any sort of causal priority on the part of the person rather than the context; the continuous feedback process between person and context is the only appropriate framework for analysis and understanding. Rather, I start with what fundamentalist people say and do, with what they believe and value. In other words, I am trying to introduce them to readers who may not have met them before and give them a voice. Analysing the ways in which their context has influenced them, and vice versa, comes at the end of the book. Informing the psychological analysis are two classical theories: those of rational choice and of social identity.

As this is a broad-ranging introductory text, I refer to secondary rather than to primary sources. I raise some questions for group discussion at the end of each brief chapter, together with a short list of further reading. Inevitably, my own experiences as a youthful fundamentalist believer and an adult social and organisational psychologist have profoundly influenced my account. However, I have tried to treat with respect the adherents of movements which are so counter-cultural that they have repeatedly suffered ridicule and abuse. *Fundamentalism continues to play an important role in the global present and future. We fail to understand it at our peril.*

References

1. Armstrong, Karen (2000) The Battle for God. London: Harper Collins.
2. Bruce, Steve (2000) Fundamentalism. Cambridge: Polity Press.

Part I
Two Fundamentalisms

1 Brethren and Taliban

Why these?

How, then, can we best be introduced to some fundamentalists? I have chosen two fundamentalist movements: the Plymouth Brethren, a Protestant Christian sect; and the Taliban, a militant Islamic movement. My reasons for these choices are varied. They both come from the Abrahamic "religions of the book". However, they also represent different ways in which fundamentalists relate to the social world: the Brethren separate themselves from it as far as possible, whereas the Taliban are actively hostile to it and seek to conquer it for Allah. The obvious and vast differences between them force us to search for the essence of fundamentalism which they hold in common.

A second reason for my choice of these two movements is that they have not been frequently featured in books about fundamentalism. We are more likely to read about the Amish or the Ultra-orthodox Jews as typifying purity and separation; and al-Qaeda or ISIS as exemplifying jihadi aggression. And finally, these two fundamentalisms, the Brethren and the Taliban, are currently active and important as part of the growth of authoritarian beliefs in an increasingly populist world. I should add at this point that the choice of the Brethren was influenced by the fact that I was brought up in a Brethren family. Readers will appreciate that this is also the reason for my interest in and feelings about fundamentalism. And finally, to repeat, a major danger of my choice of Brethren and Taliban is that it plays into the common stereotype of Islam being a more violent religion than Christianity.

However, this selection of just two movements does scant justice to the wide variety of fundamentalisms across the world. I have omitted, for example, not only Judaism but also all those fundamentalisms not based on the Abrahamic religions. There are frequent media commentaries on Hindu fundamentalism best currently exemplified in Prime Minister Modi's India, or on the extremist sects of the Buddhist and Sikh religions. My introduction to fundamentalist adherents must inevitably

DOI: 10.4324/9781003471981-3

be limited to a few examples of their belief and practice, and it inevitably does little justice to the richness and complexity of fundamentalism as a whole. I will try to compensate for this excessive selectivity by quoting examples from other fundamentalisms where appropriate.

Furthermore, fundamentalist movements are usually *sects*, that is, they have split from more mainstream elements of their religion. There is every probability that they have not given up this divisive tendency and are themselves subject to splits. Indeed, both of my chosen examples have, to a greater or lesser extent, been divided yet again into factions. The result is that my accounts of their beliefs and practices are likely to be rash generalisations which fail to do justice to their variety. But if I succeed in pointing up just a few of the key beliefs and values which they hold dear, at least readers will have experienced an initial introduction to their worldviews. And by delving into one or two of the key elements of their practice, we can put some flesh and bones on this abstract account. What, for example, do the Brethren include in their obituary notices for deceased Brothers and Sisters? And what happens in madrassahs, the educational formation of most Taliban recruits? However, at first I provide brief historical and descriptive accounts of the two movements.

The Plymouth Brethren

Readers may never have heard of the Plymouth Brethren. If they have, it may well have been the result of media accounts of financial scandal or abuse of power in a cult, part of the Exclusive sect which split from the Plymouth Brethren early in its existence. Otherwise, it is rare indeed to find any media attention directed towards the Brethren. It is also very easy not to notice their nondescript worship buildings, which used to call themselves "gospel halls", but now may be labelled simply "***** Hall", where the asterisks refer to an area or road. Or they may name themselves "evangelical church" and put a pastor's name on their notice board. What they will seldom do, however, is to describe themselves as Plymouth Brethren or anything else that might be taken as the name of a Christian denomination (e.g. Anglican or Methodist or Roman Catholic). The nearest they come to such a label is to call themselves "the assemblies". It is hardly surprising, then, that they have survived, and indeed flourished globally, for the last two hundred years in almost total obscurity.

The Brethren emerged as a splinter group from the Church of Ireland, the Anglican denomination in Ireland, in the 1820s (1). The latter part of the 18th and the early part of the 19th centuries were, of course, era of profound economic, political, social, and cultural upheaval. The idealistic founders of the movement were in tune with their radical times. They believed in the *unity* of all Christian believers. They therefore wanted freedom to worship together regardless of membership of any particular denomination with its rules and restrictions. An immediate implication was the establishment of independent and self-governing congregations. They also advocated the *priesthood* of all believers, rejecting the notion of any form of professional priesthood and emphasising instead the varied gifts of adherents. These included preaching, teaching, baptising, and administering communion, though their misleading use of the term "all believers" excluded female adherents from these tasks. The movement spread quickly in Ireland and the West of England, and by 1840 it boasted around 200 congregations. It was called Plymouth Brethren by others because a large congregation was formed in that city. However, they would only call themselves "believers" or "saints", gathered together in "the assemblies".

In the 1840s, however, the sect suffered a major schism. The *Exclusive Brethren* left the movement, led by John Nelson Derby. They rejected the independence of each congregation, and established common doctrinal and procedural rules and membership requirements across congregations. The remaining congregations became known as the *Open Brethren*. Derby went on to have a profound effect on American Protestant belief, as he preached widely in the United States about the second coming of Christ (of which, more later). However, it was the Open Brethren who flourished more in the UK throughout the 19th and into the 20th centuries. They attracted members from across the social classes, having been supported from the outset by some aristocratic and socially prominent adherents.

However, their early progressive and positive ideals began to lose their influence on their beliefs and practices. They started to emphasise what they were not, rather than what they initially wanted ideally to become. They were not a denomination, they insisted, as they defended the independence of each congregation jealously. They criticised what they termed "the sects" (i.e. the denominations) on the grounds that they were ignoring the clear instructions of Holy Scripture regarding how congregations should operate. Setting aside the freedom to worship together according to their foundational principle of the unity of all believers, they had come to embrace their own particular version of church order and discipline. They began to criticise all other Christians as apostates from the original New Testament Church and considered themselves as its only faithful adherents.

This conflict between foundational principles and subsequent separation, between generous welcome and suspicious exclusion, continued in the 20th century. Following the further growth of the middle class and suburban living, differences between suburban congregations and those in small towns and rural settings developed. The former were more

12 *Two Fundamentalisms*

likely to recognise their common grounds of belief with other evangelical Christians and to collaborate with them in such activities as the Billy Graham evangelistic missions of the 1950s. The latter, on the other hand, increasingly stressed their separation from "the sects" and the importance of adherence to what they believed to be Biblical principles of worship and church discipline.

By the 21st century, this over-simplified binary distinction was hopelessly inadequate to describe the varied diversification of the Open Brethren, let alone the multiple splits in the Exclusives. While the number of adherents in the UK has been decreasing (together with that of the mainstream Christian denominations), the Brethren have flourished in much of the rest of the world. They constitute quiet, separatist, and peaceful groups of fundamentalists who profess an authoritarian worldview to which they require close conformity (2).

The Taliban

Like the Brethren, the Taliban movement began in a period of political and cultural upheaval (3). In its case, however, this took place during late modernity, not its middle period. In the Middle East, recently established nominally Muslim nation states were mostly ruled by autocratic leaders who failed to govern on behalf of the people. Instead, they enriched themselves, fought with each other, and sometimes acted as client states of Western nations. The latter were acutely interested in the region because of its geopolitical and economic importance. In one instance of this conflict, Russia invaded Afghanistan and was defeated by local jihadist fighters aided by the United States. However, subsequently, the jihadists quarrelled among themselves, and the Taliban emerged as the opponents of the Northern Alliance of warlords. By 1996, the Taliban controlled three-quarters of Afghanistan, and ruled from 1996 to 2001, when they were overthrown by an American led North Atlantic Treaty Organisation (NATO) invasion force, on the grounds that they had supported al-Qaeda.

The word "Taliban" means students. The movement was so named because its members were recruited largely from madrassahs, or Islamic schools. They were mostly impoverished rural boys from the Pashtun tribe from the South and West of Afghanistan and received an education consisting of learning the Qu'ran by heart and a strict version of Sharia law. In power, the Taliban called Afghanistan "The First Islamic Emirate", and put Sharia law into practice. For example, they established a *ministry for "the promotion of virtue and the prevention of vice"*, which was largely concerned to enforce ultra-strict dress and behavioural codes. Violation of these rules was often punished by the lash, or sometimes by execution. Encouraged by support from Pakistan and Saudi Arabia, the Taliban acted as a safe haven for al-Qaeda and other extremist Islamic movements, which led to their invasion and defeat in 2001 by the United States and its allies.

The United States established a puppet government, led by Hamid Karzai, to replace the Taliban, but the occupying forces found themselves involved in a long and arduous campaign to defend it against a resurgent Taliban. The latter had no compunction in massacring large numbers of Afghan civilians from those areas which had previously supported their Northern Alliance enemies. They also tied down NATO forces, and in 2021, NATO. The Taliban now formed a second "Islamic Emirate", seizing control of government and reinstating the virtue and vice committee. They also completely dismantled the institutions of state established in the interim. They originally had only three political priorities: morality, commerce, and war. Given that their madrassah education had not included modern subjects of study, it is unsurprising that the state originally failed to meet the basic social, security, and economic needs of its citizens and has continued to do so in its second period in power. This impoverishment has been exacerbated by the withdrawal of Western aid in the light of the Taliban government's continued violation of women's rights. Girls were denied secondary education and removed from universities. Even the Western aid agencies seeking to prevent total destitution were forbidden from including female employees on their missions. Furthermore, a resurgent ISIS has violently destroyed the Taliban's attempt to present itself as providing control of the nation and a secure base for investment. Help from China to rebuild the ancient Silk Road for trade is still only a hopeful vision for a future not dependent on conditional Western aid.

The Deobandi tradition of militant Islam is the original ideological motivation for the Taliban's Islamic Emirate. It had developed in the 19th century to enable Muslims in India to practise their religion and obey their strict interpretation of the Sharia while living in a largely Hindu society. When Pakistan was formed at the Partition, many of the ulemas (groups of scholars of the Sharia) went there together with the Indian Muslims. In a newly formed and relatively secular nation state, these ulemas fought to gain political weight and propagate their strict Islamism. The Deobandi tradition concentrates on obedience to its interpretation of the Qu'ran and the Hadith (accounts of the Prophet Mohammed's life and sayings). While it is militant in its actions, it does not see global jihad as its primary objective, concentrating instead on ensuring conformity within its own sphere of influence. Later, however, the more militant Wahhabi tradition came to dominate the Taliban's practices.

Questions for discussion

A word of advice: please remember that everyone in the group comes from different family and social contexts. Some, like me, may have been raised in a fundamentalist family, and so may have ambivalent feelings about this experience. For others, fundamentalism will seem an utterly peculiar phenomenon. A fruitful discussion will only be possible if everyone shows respect and understanding for other participants and their stories.

1. Have you had any experience of a fundamentalist movement? If so, which movement, and what were your experiences of it? What effects, if any, did this experience have on you?
2. What stereotypes of fundamentalists are dominant in your culture or sub-culture? Where do these stereotypes come from? Which of them, if any, are you prepared to justify, and why?
3. Why do you think that fundamentalist movements are prone to split up into different sects?

References

1. Grass, Tim (2006) Gathering to his Name: The Story of Open Brethren in Britain and Ireland. Milton Keynes: Paternoster.
2. Herriot, Peter (2018) The Open Brethren: A Christian Sect in the Modern World. Cham, Switzerland: Palgrave Macmillan.
3. Kepel, Gilles (2006) Jihad: The Trail of Political Islam. London: IBTauris.

Further reading

Bruce, Steve (2000) Fundamentalism. Cambridge: Polity Press.
Lawrence, Bruce (1995) Defenders of God: The Fundamentalist Revolt against the Modern rn Age. Columbia, SC: University of South Carolina Press.

2 The Brethren
Authority and Separation

Some Brethren artefacts

So much for the history of our two sample fundamentalist movements. But what sort of people are their adherents? What are their beliefs, values, and practices, and how might we better understand them?

There are several different ways in which we might try to access fundamentalists' beliefs. The most direct is to ask them what they believe, using either structured or free-flowing interviews or questionnaires. Also, some fundamentalists have sought to make their beliefs explicit in formal propositional statements of doctrine. However, such direct evidence as this is quite difficult to come by. Further, when asked these questions, many fundamentalists might have other purposes in mind than informing the enquirer. They might, for example, be seeking to witness to the questioner in an effort to convert them; or they may be repeating what they think they ought to say as loyal adherents while privately harbouring doubts and hesitations; or they might not be in the habit of making explicit, even to themselves, what their beliefs and assumptions actually are.

There are, though, other types of evidence which enable us to infer what their beliefs are likely to be. In the case of the Brethren, these include the structure and organisation of the movement; its relationships with other religious and non-religious institutions; the nature of authority and church order and discipline; and the variety of their forms of worship (1). However, the most vivid and revealing evidence is what anthropologists refer to as *artefacts*. These are features which have a specific purpose but incidentally demonstrate the underlying beliefs on which they are based. I have selected for this purpose Brethren magazines; their individual testimonies; their obituaries; and a personal family heirloom. They permit a more personal introduction to the Brethren, giving a feel for the beliefs and values of a Brother or Sister.

I will start with what is usually considered to mark the end of a life: the *obituary* notice. The following examples are drawn from a publication entitled *The Believer's Magazine*, the readership of which tends to be drawn from the "tight" or more conservative end of the Brethren spectrum and often lives in Scotland or Northern Ireland. All were written in the second decade of the present century, and almost all refer to ordinary Brothers and Sisters rather than to particularly well-known ones.

The most obvious feature of these obituaries is their concentration on the relationship of the deceased person with their local Brethren assembly. Almost every obituary describes their *conversion*, usually a specific event when they had been saved from their sins as a result of trusting in the atoning sacrifice of Jesus Christ's crucifixion and had made public confession of this new-found faith. The absolute necessity of this conversion event applied even when the deceased had been born and brought up in a Brethren family. It enabled them to be admitted into fellowship (membership) in the assembly, provided that they gave evidence of living in accordance with their profession of repentance of their former sinful life. The other universal element of these obituaries was reference to the deceased's *faithfulness* to the assembly, as evidenced by their attendance at its regular meetings. The centrality of the assembly in their lives was also evidenced by the description of their gifts and vocations. Any reference to a "worldly" vocation, for example, a specific occupation or civic role, was rare. Instead, their "gifts of the Spirit" and their roles in the assembly took pride of place. The lengthier obituaries were of those who were "full time in the work", that is, those who were financially supported by their assembly to teach or preach full-time in the UK or as missionaries abroad.

By way of an example of faithful service, consider the nature of my father's week, once he had commuted into the City of London and done a day's work as an accountant. On Monday evening, he attended the prayer meeting and, on Wednesday, the ministry meeting (when passages of Scripture were studied). On many Saturdays he went to conferences with other local assemblies, or engaged in evangelistic activities such as distributing leaflets or preaching to the homeless in the East End of London while they ate the meal provided. On Sunday morning, it was the Breaking of Bread, the central service of Brethren practice, and in the evening, the Gospel Service (preaching for conversions). And then there were the meetings of the oversight (the church elders)..........

An important variation in these obituaries was between Brothers and Sisters. The most frequent adjective for both was "faithful". For Brothers, the next five in descending order of frequency were "consistent", "quiet", "loving", "respected", and "active". For Sisters, however, these were "hospitable", "consistent", "quiet", "interested", and "godly". The descriptor "able" was used only of Brothers, and 'meek' only of Sisters. The roles which they played in their local assembly were similarly gendered, and featured visiting the sick and elderly, teaching

Sunday School, knitting and praying for Brethren missionaries, maintaining the gospel hall, welcoming worshippers as they entered, entertaining visiting preachers, handing out leaflets, and most important, "witnessing" (seeking to convert the unsaved by one's words and actions). An interesting role was that of precentor. This was a Brother with singing ability who chose the tune and pitched the note so that the congregation could sing a hymn that had been chosen. The existence of such a role stems from the Brethren's distaste for any form of "sectarian ritual" such as the use of an organ or other musical instrument at the Breaking of Bread.

A final notable feature of the obituaries is their lengthy description of the deceased person's funeral. There is usually more than one funeral service, and the degree of esteem with which the deceased is held is reflected in the number and identity of Brothers who are "full-time in the work" who lead them. The deceased gain a great deal of respect within their assembly, among the local assemblies, and occasionally in the local community as a result of these services. Prayer is frequently asked in the obituary notice for the salvation of unsaved relatives who were present at the funeral service, and to whom the deceased was witnessing through their life's story.

Further insights into Brethren lives may be gained from the *testimonies* provided to the magazine *Assembly Testimony* by some 50 Brethren who were "full-time in the work", dating from 1997 to 2006, when the feature was discontinued. Headed "My Conversion and Call", these articles echoed some of the topics of the obituaries. In particular, harrowing accounts are provided of the feelings of acute guilt and extreme difficulty in "getting saved" in the writers' childhood. However, this pressure was also exerted regarding God's call to full-time service. The latter was contrasted with "worldly" occupations, as exemplified in the exhortation "When are you going to stop wasting your time lecturing and get on with the Lord's work?"

Given the uncertainty of "living by faith" (relying on donations from assemblies), it is hardly surprising that Brethren and Sisters wanted a clear signal from the Almighty that they should give up their current employment. Such confirmation of their call took several forms. The most frequent was the sudden occurrence in their mind of a relevant Biblical text. Or else the elders of their assembly or any older Brother might ask them if they were considering such a call; or a visa might be granted to travel to a potential field for missionary activity; or they might succeed in selling their business or house, a necessary precursor to full-time service. These mundane experiences were treated as supernatural promptings by God's Holy Spirit.

This contrast between human and divine intervention, with only the latter considered of value, is evidenced in the subsequent experience of those called to "the work". Training and planning for missionary placement, for example, was often regarded as "of man" rather than "of God". A couple reported that they "arrived in Brazil....with a two-year-old son S, little money in our pockets, knowing nobody in the land, and not speaking the Portuguese language". This is presented as "living by faith", and clearly conflicts with modern ideas of rationality, planning, and organisation. It also implies a sharp binary contrast between God and "the world", with the latter to be avoided. Values of separation and purity are clearly foremost in the worldview of those "called to the work".

The *Brethren magazines* themselves from which these obituaries and testimonies are taken constitute another interesting artefact. Particularly revealing are their titles. *Assembly Testimony* and *Believer's Magazine*, for example, imply that the Brethren are the true believers and that their truth is God's truth. Other titles, for example, *Partnership Perspectives*, *The Christian Brethren Review*, and *The Christian Brethren Research Journal* point to a very different perspective, in which the Brethren are recognised to be a denomination which can have relations with other Christians, and the academic discipline of research does not militate against faith or spirituality. These differences point up the danger of treating the Brethren as a uniform movement, when in fact it incorporates widely differing belief and value priorities.

A final artefact is a much more personal one. It is *the Bible* which I inherited from my father. It is a fine leather-bound copy, with wide margins. What makes it unusual is that on most pages the margins are filled with my father's neat accountant's hand. These entries are notes, but of a very specific kind. They consist of headings and sub-headings which essentially summarise the content of the Biblical passage next to which they appear. What is noteworthy about them is that many of them are alliterative. For example, St. Paul's famous hymn of praise to love ("charity" in the Authorised Version) in his first letter to the Corinthians is summarised as The Preeminence of Love, The Prerogatives of Love, and The Permanence of Love. Reading through these notes at length, it becomes clear that they do not add to the meaning of the passage or seek to interpret it or apply it. Rather, they are intended to increase its familiarisation and memorability.

Brethren practices

This last example is one where the artefacts and the practice of the Brethren come together. The notes in my father's Bible were designed to help him in his task as a Brother to participate in the Breaking of Bread (the service of Holy Communion). Other Brethren allowed themselves to be "guided by the Spirit" as they expounded the Scriptures, but my father liked structure and lacked confidence to speak *ex tempore*. However, my father's Bible reveals more than the Brethren mode of worship, in which male members contribute Bible passages or hymns or prayers or administration of communion "as the Spirit leads". It also points to Brethren beliefs about the nature of the Bible itself.

The purpose of my father's marginal notes was not to help his hearers to better interpret the passage of Scripture or to realise its relevance to their daily lives. To attempt this would be to arrogantly go beyond God's Word. Rather, the Bible is believed to contain within its covers everything necessary for its own interpretation. It needs no human intervention to interrupt God's direct communication with the individual believer. It is *intra-textual*, that is, it stands on its own, and even tells the believer from within its text how to read it (2). It indicates, for example, which passages are to be read as poetry or as history or as prophecy. Moreover, the gaps between the columns of print in my father's edition contained printed references to other related passages of the Bible, through which the passage concerned could be better understood.

The corollary of this belief in intra-textuality is that other texts than the Bible are extra-textual; that is, they have nothing to add to God's Word, which is itself sufficient to guide the believer into what to believe and value, and how to act. In particular, as far as the Brethren are concerned, it gives clear instructions as to how assemblies are to operate. While the Bible gives insights into how the early Christian churches functioned, and how, according to St. Paul and others, they could improve, the Brethren believe that it conveys God's instructions to believers everywhere and in every era.

A wide variety of other practices also point to Brethren beliefs and values. Consider, for example, the exercise of *authority* within each assembly and the rules of church order and discipline. The Brethren believe that their own mode of governance accords with that of the early church. They are upholding a tradition handed down from that golden age by a faithful few throughout the church's history. Rewards and punishments are ultimately administered by God himself at the day of judgement. However, in the meantime church governance and discipline are administered by the elders. They pay much attention to various admonitions of St. Paul to the early churches, which often involve how Sisters should act. Unsurprisingly, these exemplify the patriarchal culture of their era, with high values on female modesty and subservience. The consequence is that a surprising amount of attention is paid to female dress and the modest covering of their hair. Furthermore, Sisters are not permitted to give utterance at the Breaking of Bread, and are expected to play a subordinate role in family life, submitting gladly to male headship.

Two Fundamentalisms

Or consider the Brethren's relationship with *the world*. The world is defined as the social systems of modernity, which are "of man" and not "of God". The only approved worldly system is that of "the powers that be", that is, the rulers whom God has appointed to exercise authority. Consequently, Brethren interact as little as possible with social systems such as the arts, media, science, and politics. They are particularly concerned about their children going to university and studying those subjects which might lead them to question their faith.

But they are not only concerned to maintain their purity by separating themselves from "the world". They are also wary of *"the sects"*, that is, all other Christian denominations or movements. The label is significant: everyone else is "sectarian" because they have failed to follow God's instructions for the church, being seduced by the attractions of liturgy or priesthood. But the most dangerous enemies of all are *"the apostates"*, that is, people who know the truth but deliberately reject it. This is code for Brethren who have fallen away from the truth. Since it is easy to come to different conclusions about what God is actually saying to the believer in his Word, apostates who hold some different beliefs to one's own are a constant danger. They are considered to be sent by Satan to sow seeds of doubt and disbelief in assemblies, and to challenge the will of the Holy Spirit as revealed to the elders. An artefact which indicates the prevalence of this anxiety to defend the assembly's purity of doctrine and teaching is the "letter of commendation". When my parents went on holiday and sought to worship at the local assembly, they took with them a letter signed by the elders of their own assembly to vouchsafe for their soundness of doctrine and godly lives.

Once again, however, it is important to note that these artefacts and practices are to be found to markedly different degrees in the Brethren (3). Many assemblies collaborate happily with other local Christians on occasion, and tolerate a degree of divergence of opinion on debated theology. This is precisely what one would expect when each assembly is avowedly self-governing and is located in different sub-cultures in national and global society. Nevertheless, the more conservative and absolutist practices continue to be prevalent in many assemblies today.

Questions for discussion

1. What have you read in this chapter that surprised you most about the Brethren? Why do you think it surprised you? How does it make you feel about them?
2. On the basis of what you have read in this chapter, what would you consider to be the three most important beliefs or values for the Brethren? Why do you think these are important to them?

3 Why have the Brethren survived and prospered for two hundred years?
4 How do you think a conservative Brother or Sister would respond to this chapter?

References

1. Herriot, Peter (2018) The Open Brethren: A Christian Sect in the Modern World. Cham: Palgrave Macmillan.
2. Hood, Ralph, Hill, Peter, & Williamson, Paul (2005) The Psychology of Religious Fundamentalism. New York, NY: Guilford.
3. Grass, Tim (2006) Gathering to his Name: The Story of Open Brethren in Britain and Ireland. Milton Keynes: Paternoster.

3 The Taliban
Sharia and Jihad

Two artefacts

The Taliban can only be understood in terms of their geographical and cultural context, in which they are deeply rooted. They are primarily drawn from the Pashtun tribe, which is located mainly in the southern parts of Afghanistan. Thus, unlike some other Islamic movements, adherents are already related by local and family ties and by a shared history and culture. The first artefact I will review, which stems from this context, is their system of *madrassahs*. These are schools (the word is used of all Islamic schools), but Taliban madrassahs have particular characteristics (1).

They are boarding schools which provide free board and teaching for impoverished and mostly rural children whose parents could not afford to provide them with an education, or sometimes even adequate sustenance. They are almost entirely closed systems, in which students form close ties with each other and with their teachers, and have little contact with anyone outside the school. They study the Qu'ran, the Hadith (the reported words of the Prophet Mohammed), and the Sunnah (his reported actions). Much of the curriculum consists of learning by heart passages of these documents, despite their being written in Arabic, not the students' native language. Other non-religious disciplines, for example, sciences, are generally avoided because they are associated with the godless West.

When the outside world does enter the madrassah, it is often in the form of visiting Taliban clergy, who encourage jihad and martyrdom and teach such assertions as "a woman not wearing a veil causes prostitution". In general, an exclusive identity of "us versus them" is inculcated, with 'them' defined as "unbelievers". This term does not only refer to those of other religions or none, but also to other Muslims, such as the Shia or Sufi branches of Islam. At one popular girls' madrassah, the emphasis on purity and separation from the world of unbelievers is exemplified by the prohibition of radio, television, social media, and photographs. Male teachers work from behind a curtain so as to avoid eye contact with students (2).

As a consequence of this mode of education, employment opportunities for madrassah graduates are limited in the extreme. Many become members of the Taliban's army of jihadi warriors, or else go back to a madrassah and teach. As a reporter puts it, referring to a teacher in a madrassah, "(t)he world is his room". Even in a theocracy such as Afghanistan or Iran, the successful function of government to provide security and services is dependent on the existence of a more broadly educated citizen body than the graduates of madrassahs.

The second Taliban artefact of interest is the *committee for the propagation of virtue and the prevention of vice*. Much media attention has understandably been paid to this body's insistence on women wearing clothing which accords with strict Islamic rules relating to female "modesty". Reports also stress the public beatings administered to women who are adjudged by the agents of the committee to have broken these rules. Attention has also focused on the other ways in which women's lives are restricted. They are excluded from university education and from almost all occupations except nursing and teaching. The evidence of female witnesses in courts is allocated only half the weight allocated to males. Women are often subjected to domestic violence in accordance with the admonition of the Qu'ran: "As for those [women] from whom you fear disobedience, admonish them, and send them to beds apart, and beat them" (3).

Discrimination against women is, of course, typical of patriarchal forms of religion. It is particularly apparent in theocracies because it is incorporated into their legal systems and officially enforced. In Afghanistan, therefore, it is not merely a cultural feature especially likely to be found in pre-modern societies. Clearly, its treatment of women is of fundamental importance to understanding the Taliban. However, the committee is not primarily concerned with enforcing rules specifically relating to women. Rather, its remit is to police an immense range of religious and social behaviour. For example, it paints over murals and destroys representational art and cultural objects such as statues of the Buddha and even some ornamentation in mosques. It bans a whole range of popular entertainments and recreational pastimes. It discriminates against persons of other religions and is particularly severe on "apostates", that is, those who do not practice Islamic worship in the approved way. It forbids all forms of sexual activity except marital sex and can punish violations with extreme sanctions, including, on occasion, stoning to death. Other sanctions are equally extreme, for example, amputation as a punishment for some types of theft. In sum, the committee enforces obedience to a wide range of detailed prohibitions which constitute near total surveillance and control of citizens' lives.

Sharia and Jihad

A third Taliban artefact which I want to explore is their ideology regarding *Sharia Law and Jihad* (4). An ideology is a dogmatic theoretical narrative which is designed both to justify and to motivate. What sort of ideology can justify the practices implied by the first two artefacts, madrassahs and the committee? And how can Afghan citizens be motivated, at the very least, to comply with the controls and limitations imposed upon them, let alone to assent and conform voluntarily? A grossly over-simplified and anglicised version of Taliban ideology might run as follows:

> Allah himself used the angel Gabriel to dictate his words to the Prophet Mohammed in the form of the Qu'ran. And the Prophet himself spoke and acted in a similarly inspired way. These three sources, the Qur'an, the Hadith, and the Sunnah, constitute the only necessary and sufficient authority for true believers to guide their beliefs and their practices regarding worship and social relations.
>
> Sharia is the body of laws which expound these authoritative requirements. Sharia is eternal and unchangeable, but from the earliest times of the Prophet, it has been interpreted by scholars and clergy so that it may be better understood by every believer. Sharia has to be obeyed to the letter, and it both mandates some actions and forbids others. It also specifies how violations are to be sanctioned.
>
> Individuals are not equal in the eyes of the law, since Allah has ordained that men and women are to be treated differently, as are believers and infidels. Indeed, believers are urged to engage in Jihad, the eternal struggle against infidels in defence of Islam. Infidels include not only adherents of other religions or none, but also apostates. These are Muslims who have failed to honour and obey the Sharia. They are guilty of such sins as ornamentation in mosques; veneration of saints, not of Allah alone; and a proliferation of priests intervening between the believer and Allah. None of these practices is permitted by the true Sharia, based on the Qu'ran, Hadith, and Sunnah alone. They are, however, rife among Shi'a and Sufi Muslims, who are consequently apostates from the true faith. In the early years of Islam, its golden age, the true Sharia was practised. It is now revived and being implemented in the Afghan Emirate.

Identity, separation, and control

These artefacts point clearly to three general features of the Taliban movement (5). First, it establishes a strong identity for its adherents, by characterising them as the (only true) believers. Second, it presents them with a simple binary worldview: a conflict between believers and infidels. And third, it exercises tight control over social and religious life by enforcing its version of God's law. It characterises its own beliefs and practices as the foundational Islamic faith as revealed to the Prophet Mohammed.

In fact, the Taliban version of Islam is the mixed product of various modern reactionary movements usually labelled "Salafist". The first of these is the Deobandi tradition, which sought to give Indian Muslims a clear identity when they were a minority before Partition. After that event, many Deobandi clergy went to the new nation of Pakistan and neighbouring Afghanistan, and established madrassahs there. They exercised considerable political influence in their new national homes, and when the Taliban were founded, they constituted its religious base. However, they were strongly influenced by the Wahaabi movement, which was based primarily in Saudi Arabia (the Taliban and their madrassahs received a great deal of financial support from the Saudis). The strict and dogmatic Wahaabi insistence on a literal interpretation of Sharia law soon dominated the somewhat more nuanced Deobandi version, and the Taliban ideology summarised above owes more to Wahaabi than to Deobandi influence.

A final contribution to this ideology follows from the movement's roots in the Pashtun tribe. Two features of Pashtun culture valued highly are, first, personal, family, and tribal honour and dignity; and second, revenge for perceived insult or damage. This contribution adds emotional and motivational power to the struggle between us and them, believers and infidels, the Taliban and the evil world. While other Salafist movements have lost prominence in very recent years, the Taliban have regained their position as rulers of one of the two avowed Muslim theocracies. Their use of their version of Sharia to ensure compliance internally and their fostering of the idea of Jihad to stir up conflict have enabled them to gain and maintain a strong locally-based movement.

Peculiarly different?

By now, many readers may be feeling that the Brethren and the Taliban are indeed very strange and unusual people. It is easy to regard people who take their religion very seriously and who appear not to be living in the same (late modern) world as us as totally different. However, I argue throughout this book that fundamentalists are not uniquely different from the rest of us.

First, there are many other people whose time and effort are largely devoted to only one of the great social systems of the world. For the fundamentalist, this is, of course, religion. But for others, it may be science or politics or art or media or business, for example. Many are "single-minded" in their perspective, and modernity with its continuous differentiation of its social systems makes it more likely that they will know "more and more about less and less" (6).

Furthermore, global social systems, such as religion, and social institutions and movements within them, such as the Brethren and the Taliban, exist and prosper because they meet many of the universal and fundamental needs of humankind. They provide meaning to our existence, fostering beliefs and values that shape our worldview and guide our intentions and actions. They add to our self-esteem, enabling us to see ourselves as having value as a person, and exercising agency and choice in our lives. They meet our needs for affiliation and membership, and give us a social identity (7), the possibility of thinking of ourselves as true believers. Other social systems permit us to think of ourselves as creative artists, or innovative scientists, or patriotic citizens. What's more, all of these social systems and their sub-systems, including religion, operate through the same basic *social processes*: the acquisition of influence and power, for example, and the exercise of leadership; the distinctiveness of particular social groups, particularly those whose members conform closely to a set of norms of behaviour; the processes of collaboration, competition, or hostility with other social systems; and so on.

However, we tend not to approach fundamentalists from the perspective of their similarities to ourselves. Rather, we look at the differences, particularly those of which we disapprove. They are absolutists, we judge, believing themselves to be right and everyone else wrong. They are separatists, having as little as possible to do with everyone else. They are hopelessly stuck in the past, in a pre-modern view of the world. It may well appear that relative to late-modern industrial and post-industrial cultures, fundamentalists *are* out of step. But once again, we should note that they are not on their own in these perceived shortcomings. There is currently an increase in nationalist populist absolutism (8), which discounts any other perspective. There is extreme polarisation, both within and between nation states. And there is a widespread harking back to a supposed golden age in the past.

Fundamentalists, then, cannot be understood in terms of a strange other. We can only hope to understand them if we use the same methods and concepts which we employ to understand ourselves.

Questions for discussion

1 Why do you think the Taliban have been so successful relative to other Islamist movements?
2 What are the main ways in which the Taliban and the Brethren differ from each other?
3 What are the main ways in which they resemble each other?

References

1. *Financial Times*, October 30th 2015. Madrassas: behind closed doors
2. www.bbc.co.uk/news/world-asia-Z6418558
3. Qu'ran chapter 4 (Women) verse 34
4. Kepel, Gilles (2006) Jihad: The Trail of Political Islam (5th edn.) London: IBTauris
5. Silinsky, Mark (2014) The Taliban: Afghanistan's Most Lethal Insurgents. New York, NY: Barnes & Noble
6. Beyer, Peter (2006) Religions in Global Society. London: Routledge
7. Jenkins, Richard (2008) Social Identity (3rd edn.) London: Routledge
8. Mudde, Cas & Kaltwasser, Cristobal (2017) Populism: A Very Short Introduction. New York, NY: Oxford University Press

Further reading

Armstrong, Karen (2001) Islam: A Short History. London: Phoenix

Gerges, Fawaz (2005) The Far Enemy: Why Jihad Went Global. New York: Cambridge University Press

Rashid, Ahmed (2000) Taliban: Islam, Oil, and the New Great Game in Central Asia. London: IBTauris.

Part II
Fundamentalist Beliefs

4 God's Word

The importance of belief

Having briefly reviewed two of the many current fundamentalisms by way of initial familiarisation, we need to be more intimately introduced to fundamentalists themselves. Taking a social psychological perspective, I could start from either end of the spectrum, the social or the psychological. But, to repeat, this is a matter of emphasis; the social and the psychological are not mutually exclusive alternative explanations, but both are parts of the same dynamic interaction. Their context acts upon individuals, and individuals act upon their context. Most books on fundamentalism start with its social and cultural context, however, with the result that the analysis of fundamentalists as individual actors and agents may be downplayed.

So, why is this second part of the book titled "Fundamentalist *Beliefs*"? Why, in other words, have I singled out one aspect of their psychology at the expense of others? Surely, you might object, the main differentiating feature of fundamentalists is their personality, or their prejudices, or their emotions. However, a traditional psychological framework based on the proposition that *action is primarily based upon belief* is the one which best explains their behaviour and practices (1). It suggests that their actions are derived from and motivated by their beliefs and their value priorities (a particular form of belief). Social norms then come into play. These norms may discourage people from carrying out the actions which their beliefs imply (or they may further encourage them to act). Of course, a wide range of other factors impact upon whether intentions to act are carried out in practice or not. Primary among these are fundamentalists' motivational commitment and emotional involvement, which are enhanced by the narratives they hear. Another factor is situational – they may simply not have the opportunity to act in accordance with their beliefs. If a person is in prison, for example, they may be unable to carry out what they perceive to be their religious duties. And finally, to repeat, rational choice theory treats only one direction of the belief-action-outcome-belief cycle, rather than dealing with the dynamic interaction of person and context. The theory is relevant at this point because I have prioritised the belief-action part of the cycle in the major part of the book.

By using this explanatory framework, one is taking at face value fundamentalists' assertion that their actions follow from their beliefs. In other words, while we may not ourselves accept their beliefs as rational or true, we might agree that their intentions and actions follow from them. It is worth noting that this emphasis on beliefs giving rise to actions is contrary to the frequent assumption that beliefs are simply spoken or unspoken justifications for past or intended actions. Of course, the need to justify our actions to others and the opportunity to do so in high-minded terms are part and parcel of political, legal, and social life. But to attribute this motive to all beliefs, implicit or explicit, is a highly partial account.

How, then, may we discover what fundamentalists' beliefs are? Often, they seek to tell us explicitly in the form of doctrinal statements or ideological narratives, although these often serve the purpose of instruction or motivation for adherents rather than information to others. However, as I have sought to show in the previous two chapters, we can infer their beliefs from their artefacts (using this term in its widest sense). I will argue that there are two core beliefs upon which fundamentalist belief systems rest. These are, first, that *God tells individual believers through his Word all they need to know about what they should believe and how they should act* (2). And second, that *there exists a constant cosmic conflict between God and Satan, acted out in a continuing struggle between believers and unbelievers* (3).

It is immediately clear that these expressions of beliefs are written in terms which assume there is one God, that he expresses himself through his Word, and that his enemy is Satan. In other words, I am writing from a cultural religious background of monotheism, sacred text, and evil spiritual adversary. If I were to try to formulate more broadly based versions of these two core beliefs, they might contain such terms as "the transcendent". My only excuses for using the language of the three Abrahamic religions, Judaism, Christianity, and Islam, are first, that it informs my own cultural heritage; second, that most of the movements generally categorised as "fundamentalist" are derived from them; and finally, that most of my readers are likely to have this same cultural background.

These two core beliefs emerge clearly from my accounts of the Brethren and the Taliban. The Brethren base their church practice and their family life on what they believe are God's instructions to them, especially those to be found in the latter parts of the New Testament. The Taliban enforce a strict behavioural code derived from interpretations of the Qu'ran. And in terms of conflict, the Brethren denounce the evil world and spiritual apostasy while seeking to keep pure and separate from them. The Taliban, on the other hand, try to vanquish infidels on Allah's behalf. But both are trying to obey God's Word and to struggle with evil. The same two core beliefs characterise other fundamentalisms as well. This is a bold claim, but one which I hope will be supported by the examples which I cite throughout the text.

Clearly, the notion of "core" beliefs implies that there are "secondary" beliefs. While the two core beliefs and their immediate implications are common to fundamentalisms, their numerous secondary ones differ markedly. Indeed, one can discern a number of different belief dimensions on which some fundamentalisms take a position at the polar opposite to others. In this chapter, I will explore the first core belief: the total authority of the Word of God; in the next, the worldview of cosmic conflict; and in chapter 6, secondary beliefs in terms of their variety and outcomes.

The Word of God

So, we might wonder, what is so unusual about religious people giving great authority to their holy books? Certainly, the three Abrahamic religions all do so. Indeed, they are known as "the religions of the book" for precisely this reason. The total authority which fundamentalists give to their book is, however, of a completely different order from that of mainstream believers. In mainstream religion, there are several different sources of religious authority and revelation. While the holy book is one of these, others include religious tradition, human reason, the natural world, personal religious experience, and ecclesiastical authority. If we unpack the statement of the first core fundamentalist belief, the difference between fundamentalisms and mainstream may become clearer. The key to appreciating the fundamentalists' approach to God's Word is to grasp the relationship which they propose between God and his Word. The Word is understood to be the expression of God himself, the means by which he has revealed himself. *Whatever God is, the Word is, and to deny the Word is therefore to deny God* (4).

Now God is omniscient, eternal, and omnipotent, so his Word has to express these characteristics. Thus, if God is *omniscient*, then the Word has to equally comprehensive in its scope. It has to contain all that believers need to know about what is true and should be believed, and what is good and should be acted upon. It is adept at communicating such truths and at pointing up the contrasting falsehoods and sins of unbelievers. The Word is entirely sufficient to the extent that it is *intratextual*; that is, there is no need to go outside it. It even tells you how to read it (whether, for example, a passage is to be read as poetry, history, law, or prophecy). Moreover, God's omniscience implies that his Word is inerrant, in the sense that it is internally consistent. So, for example, the fact that there are contradictions in different accounts of the same event has to be explained away by the proposal that the accounts are actually of different events (5). Fundamentalists do not, however, believe in the literal truth of the Word, for they distinguish between different genres, some of which are figurative, for example, history and poetry.

God is also *eternal*, from everlasting to everlasting, always the same. Therefore, his Word is similarly unchanging, having been revealed to humankind in a past golden age. The Word is eternally true; its meaning has never changed. It is absolutely true, whatever the context. All other "truth", whether historical or scientific or artistic, is relative, fallible, and human in origin. Only God's revealed Word is eternal, final, and absolute. And God is *omnipotent*. He wields universal and absolute power. There are no rivals, as even the ubiquitous Satan's fate is ultimately sealed. The Word, therefore, has to express the Almighty's power. Its truth and holiness destroy not only the ungodly and infidel world's systems but also all false religion and apostasy.

Finally, the very fact that God has chosen to reveal himself in his Word carries immense implications. Indeed, we would not know that he is omniscient, eternal, and omnipotent if the Word had not told us so. Because we know that the Word is the complete revelation of God, we can accept it as a unified whole with a single structure. All its parts are related and can throw light on each other. It is God alone who has revealed himself in this way, and the human authors are simply the channels he has used for the purpose. Moses came down from Sinai with the Torah which God had given him (6). The prophet Mohammed received the Qu'ran as dictated to him by the angel Gabriel, sent by God for that very purpose (7). The authors of the books of the Bible were who the Bible says they were, and each of them was inspired by God's Holy Spirit (8).

Further, God is communicating directly with the believer through his Word. While some believers are more ready than others to receive the revelation, it is comprehensible to all. God is graciously revealing himself to us and requires no complex logic or intuition on our part. We simply have to submit to the supernatural, rather than striving as "natural man" to work things out for ourselves. Indeed, we should understand the world in supernatural terms. God and Satan are engaged in spiritual warfare, with all its consequences for humankind.

While these fundamentalist beliefs are based upon the idea of their religion's holy book constituting God's Word, the first core belief could be held by fundamentalists other than those from the Abrahamic religions. In their case, the term "Word" could be extended to cover a variety of modes of expression of God or gods, for example, the words or performative actions of charismatic movement leaders.

Belief and experience

Their core belief in God's Word is typical of fundamentalists' beliefs, values, and norms of behaviour in general. The belief and its associated implications as outlined above are couched in starkly binary terms, with one term overwhelming the other (9). The Word is supernaturally revealed, not naturally discovered. The Word is the only way by which God may be known and the truth understood; all other social systems are human inventions, which are unnecessary and mistaken if they do not reflect revealed truth. God's Word is unchanging and timeless; hence, any changes over time in its accepted meaning and interpretation are misguided and untrue. And it is coherent and comprehensible to believers if they read it humbly and obediently and are ready to hear what the Almighty has to say to them. It is not composed by multiple human voices with different narratives to tell.

Yet fundamentalists might find it difficult to ignore several of their experiences, which argue against this first core belief and its implications. For example, different believers habitually arrive at *different interpretations* of the Word. As a result, they frequently leave the fundamentalist movement of which they were adherents and form a new movement or sect. As we have seen, this sectarian split happened early in the history of the Brethren and repeatedly thereafter. It also characterises militant Islamic organisations and ultra-orthodox Jews. It is difficult to square with the belief that God's Word is clearly expressed so that it is revealed in its entirety to ordinary believers. Why, in that case, are different interpretations so common?

Moreover, *fundamentalists are themselves modern people*. They cannot therefore avoid involvement in modern social systems other than religion – science, media, education, law, government, business, and so on (10). This makes it very hard for them to act on the basis that everything they need to know is to be found in God's Word and that other social systems are mere human inventions and likely to be incompatible with it. Instead, they frequently seek to use these systems to try to prove its truth. For example, there is an extensive Protestant fundamentalist literature seeking to prove the scientific possibility and historic fact of Christ's resurrection. This marshals non-Biblical methods and concepts, a strategy incompatible with the belief that the only reason that we should believe in the resurrection is that the Bible tells us about it.

Not only do different believers have different interpretations of the Word. Also, the interpretations which fundamentalist movements hold to be true *change over time*. So, for example, the concept of Jihad, the attempted conquest of Satan in the Islamist believer's own environment, including his own soul, became a justification for revolution against nominally Muslim governments, and finally for assaults on the Great

Satan, the liberal Western world (11). In order for the Islamic fundamentalists to achieve their leaders' vision, they had to accept a change in the beliefs, which justified and motivated their actions. In the United States in the 1980s, the fundamentalist leader Jerry Falwell persuaded fundamentalist believers to ally with Evangelicals to fight against secularism in American society. This required them to change their definitions of apostasy (now no longer to include the Evangelicals) and of this evil world (no longer American politics) (12). And finally, some ultra-orthodox Jews have now construed the return of the Messiah to consist of the return of the nation of Israel to occupy the entire territory promised to them by their forefather Abraham (13).

However, despite these apparently disconfirming experiences, fundamentalists do not seem to have too much difficulty in retaining their first core belief and its implications. There are many possible explanations for this continuing adherence, some of which I explore at length in later chapters. In particular, the retention of both of the two core beliefs meets several basic psychological needs. Furthermore, their mutually confirming relationship provides a total world view and the individual believer's place within it. What is vitally important for fundamentalist movements is that the core beliefs of their adherents generate, motivate, and justify those intentions and actions which achieve their aims.

Questions for discussion

1 What are the major obstacles which typically prevent religious beliefs being realised in action?
2 What are the defining features of the modern world? To what extent if any are they compatible with the first core belief of fundamentalists?
3 Is divine revelation the binary opposite of human discovery? Why and how might fundamentalists try to reconcile the two?

References

1. Fishbein, Martin, & Ajzen, Icek (1975) Belief, Attitude, Intention, and Behavior. New York: Addison-Wesley.
2. Hood, Ralph, Hill, Peter, & Williamson, Paul (2005) The Psychology of Religious Fundamentalism. New York: Guilford.
3. Brekke, Torkel (2012) Fundamentalism: Prophecy and Protest in an Age of Globalization. New York: Cambridge University Press.
4. Lawrence, Bruce (1989) Defenders of God: The Fundamentalist Revolt Against the Modern Age. Columbia, SC: University of South Carolina Press.
5. Barr, James (1977) Fundamentalism. London: SCM Press.
6. Schimmel, Solomon (2008) The Tenacity of Unreasonable Beliefs: Fundamentalism and the Fear of Truth. New York: Oxford University Press.

7. Armstrong, Karen (2006) Muhammad: Prophet for Our Time. London: Harper Collins.
8. Carpenter, Joel (1997) Revive Us Again: The Reawakening of American Fundamentalism. New York: Oxford University Press.
9. Almond, Gabriel, Appleby, Scott, & Sivan, Emmanuel (2003) Strong Religion: The Rise of Fundamentalisms around the World. Chicago: University of Chicago Press.
10. Beyer, Peter (2006) Religions in Global Society. London: Routledge.
11. Gerges, Fawaz (2005) The Far Enemy: Why Jihad Went Global. Cambridge: Cambridge University Press.
12. Harding, Susan (2000) The Book of Jerry Falwell: Fundamentalist Language and Politics. Princeton, NJ: Princeton University Press.
13. Aran, Gideon (1991) Jewish Zionist fundamentalism: The bloc of the faithful in Israel (Gush Emunim). In Marty Martin, Appleby Scott (eds.) Fundamentalisms Observed. Chicago: Chicago University Press.

Further Reading

Hood, Ralph, Hill, Peter, & Williamson, Paul (2005) The Psychology of Religious Fundamentalism. New York: Guilford.

Brekke, Torkel (2012) Fundamentalism: Prophecy and Protest in an Age of Globalization. New York: Cambridge University Press.

Herriot, Peter (2009) Religious Fundamentalism: Global, Local, and Personal. London: Routledge.

5 Cosmic War

Binaries

Fundamentalist belief is full of binary distinctions (1). The basic binary contrast in the previous chapter was between divine revelation and human discovery, God's Word versus modern ideas. The second core belief of fundamentalists, the *world-view of constant conflict and struggle*, is implied by several more such binaries. The most fundamental of these is between God and Satan, good and evil. Other powerful pairs of opposites are, for example, believer and unbeliever, spiritual and carnal, godly and worldly, pure and defiled, obedient and rebellious, and observant and careless.

For the fundamentalist believer, the first term of all of these binaries is valued highly, and the second hated and feared. As believers, they of course identify as followers of God and targets of Satan's wiles, faithful to the Almighty but tempted by sin. They also distinguish themselves from all those who are not fellow adherents of their particular fundamentalism. However, there are various categories of those they call unbelievers (2). The first group is those of *other religions or none*: "infidels" or "heathen" or "gentiles" or "secularists". The second are those of *the same religion* as the fundamentalists, but in their view have lapsed into purely "nominal" religious observance. Members of this category would call themselves mainstream. And the third category consists of *other fundamentalist sects*, which differ from the fundamentalism in question, sometimes having split from it over differences which to outsiders might appear of minor significance.

Examples of these three different categories abound. For the Brethren, for example, social institutions are "the world", mainstream Christian denominations are "the sects", and disaffected Brethren are "apostates" or "unsound". For the Taliban, the West is "the Great Satan", Muslim nations are "apostate", and other radical Islamist movements, such as ISIS or al-Qaeda, are rivals. All unbelievers are at fault. For Protestant Christian fundamentalists, their primary error is unbelief or false belief, in other words, heterodoxy. In the opinion of militant Islamists and ultra-orthodox Jews, however, unbelievers fail to properly obey the Sharia or the Torah. Their sin is of practice more than belief, heteropraxis (3).

So much for the first two binaries of the list of seven, selected from among many, which I suggested above: God and Satan, and believer and unbeliever. The others are similarly dichotomies of white versus black; shades of grey are not entertained. The remaining five examples are, to repeat: spiritual versus carnal, godly versus worldly, pure versus defiled, obedient versus rebellious, and observant versus careless. Fundamentalists believe that God has revealed to them through his Word that the true believer should strive for the first term of these dichotomies and abhor the second. *Since the central identity of fundamentalists is as a believer*, then they must ensure they themselves are spiritual, godly, pure, obedient, and observant. Conversely, they should abhor what is carnal, worldly, defiled, rebellious, and careless.

Once again, it is easy to spot examples of fundamentalists seeking to establish themselves as obedient believers in these respects. They may build figurative or indeed literal *boundaries* around themselves. For example, ultra-orthodox Jews may draw physical boundary markers round their communities and seek to ensure that their interpretation of the Torah is obeyed to the letter within them. A considerable proportion of ultra-orthodox males spend their adult lives studying the Torah to ensure that they understand and obey it. The Amish live in separate communities and shun adherents who break the rules regarding dealings with "the world" (4). All fundamentalisms require women to wear clothes which conceal much or nearly all of their bodies. Failing to observe the smallest regulation can result in immediate physical beating by the Taliban's committee for vice and virtue (note the dualism). Secular education is treated with deep suspicion by fundamentalists for fear that Satan may infiltrate and corrupt the believing family, and the same is true of the arts. Further, friendship with unbelievers (that is, all non-adherents) is discouraged. The only exception is when the friend is cultivated by the believer in an effort to convert them. The Brethren require visitors from another assembly to show a letter of commendation, indicating that they are sound in life and doctrine and will not introduce false teaching, and so on.

Now the binaries which I have discussed are abstract terms relating to concepts of morality and purity, belief and value (the one exception being the supernatural actors, God and Satan). However, the binaries are also likely to be related to *believers' identity and self-concept*. If they identify as believers, then they will also perceive themselves to possess the defining features of believers. While they may not consider themselves to have fully achieved these virtues, they are likely to have in their minds a *prototype* of the ideal believer to which they aspire and which their leaders embody. But what of the opposite terms of the binaries, for example, carnality, worldliness, defilement, rebelliousness, and carelessness? These too are likely to be perceived by fundamentalist believers as characteristics of categories of people. They can label these categories as "the world", or "infidels", or "apostates", and then they can *stereotype* all members of these categories as worldly, sinful, etc (5).

The outcome of this binary belief system is the conflictual "Us versus Them". The cosmic spiritual battle between God and Satan is expressed and reflected in this ongoing struggle between believers and unbelievers. The good in the world is attributed to God and the believers, the bad to Satan and the unbelievers. The struggle may be conducted in very different ways, depending on whether the fundamentalism in question is motivated more by fear or by anger. Some fundamentalisms separate themselves from Them for fear of becoming impure through contamination. Others attack Them physically or politically out of anger at their sinfulness. However, these different modes of conflict are based on secondary beliefs, stemming from the second core belief shared by all fundamentalists that there is a cosmic war being waged between God and Satan, which is reflected in the conflicts between believers and unbelievers.

Dramatic narrative

The history of this conflict, its present status, and its likely future outcomes are dramatised by fundamentalisms by narrative stories, all with a single simple structure (6). First, in a glorious and *golden past age*, God revealed himself. For the Jews, he rescued them from slavery, gave the Torah to Moses on Mount Sinai, and established them in the promised land of Judaea and Samaria. For Christians, the golden age encompassed the teaching, crucifixion, resurrection, and ascension of Christ, the inspired mission of the disciples, and the establishment of the early churches. And for Muslims the revelation of the Qu'ran to the Prophet Mohammed via the angel Gabriel and the establishment of the caliphate constituted the glorious beginnings of their religion.

Soon, however, runs the narrative, Satan corrupted the purity and splendour of this golden age. Many forms of heresy and disobedience threatened the true believers, the *remnant* of the original adherents. Often only a faithful few continued to believe and obey God's Word, despite the persecution they suffered for their faithfulness. Threats to the truth have continued to the present day, and indeed, appear to have reached a dreadful *climax* in this present sinful age. Never has man's rebellion against God been so brazen as it is at present, to the extent that the very existence of true religion is threatened (7). Faced with such a crisis, the only proper response is to seek to ensure its survival. This can be achieved either by *separating* completely from this evil world and remaining pure and undefiled; or by *fighting* against it and overcoming it with the Almighty's help.

The fundamentalisms derived from the Abrahamic religions use mostly different historical events, heroes, and villains as the cast for this dramatic story line. However, they are all motivated by the same supposed existential threat. This has been engineered by Satan himself and constituted by enemies, for example, the sinful West with its liberal democracies and sexual depravity; nation states nominally Muslim but in thrall to the West; and mysterious international networks such as the New World Order or other global or local conspiracies. And there are always those who betray the believers from within their ranks, seduced by Satan to sow seeds of heresy and discord.

The struggle will be hard, but it will conclude soon enough. The true believers will be victorious, led by the Messiah or a heroic leader from the golden age. They will rule on God's behalf, and the glories of the original golden age will be restored. God's commands will be obeyed in all their detail, and the world will be pure and righteous once again (8).

Now this epic story of conflict and victory is clearly based on the second core belief - that *the world is the stage for the cosmic conflict between God and Satan* and between their respective followers. Their self-identification as the only true believers in their God results in a world-view in which they see themselves as virtuous and all others as a generalised sinful Other, with the inevitable result being a continuous conflict between Us and Them. The function of the narrative is to enable believers to see themselves as fighting on the winning side, and to be strongly motivated to struggle without ceasing. Clearly, the narrative contains many secondary beliefs, but it is rooted in the second core fundamentalist belief in cosmic conflict.

Differentiation and conformity

This fundamentalist narrative framework, although using some different vocabulary, is available to all fundamentalisms. However, not all of them succeed in maintaining their initial impetus. Some fail to retain their adherents or attract new ones, despite the high drama of their narratives. Others survive largely by maintaining very high birth rates (the ultra-orthodox Haredim and the Amish, for example). But neither reproductive fertility nor powerful narrative are sufficient by themselves to prevent many fundamentalist sects and movements from fading away. Of course, there are economic, political, and social factors which have a profound effect on their survival rate. However, a theoretical framework helps to at least partly explain why some fade away and others stick with the struggle. It runs as follows (9).

Any social system needs to be able to *differentiate* itself from all other social systems if it is to have an independent existence. It needs to possess certain features which distinguish it and make it both identifiable and also desirable. At the physical level, many fundamentalisms differentiate themselves by their public appearance and behaviour. The Haredim wear unusual clothing and hairstyles. The Taliban ride around in pick-up trucks carrying guns. The Brethren carry their Bibles to assembly meetings. At the level of belief and ritual practice, too, fundamentalisms demonstrate their differences from other sects loudly and clearly. This is often because they have frequently split from other religious systems as a result of disagreement about such matters. Since this differentiating feature was the cause of the split, it is very important to emphasise its centrality for the movement and give adherents a reason for the sect's independent existence. However, to observers it may be surprising that such apparently trivial differences can justify a fundamentalism's existence.

Fundamentalisms also have to differentiate themselves from much larger enemies. All non-believers constitute the Other to whom they are opposed. Since they themselves are the only true believers, their task is to demonstrate how different they are from the rest of the world. One major differentiator is their scrupulous obedience to God. They themselves strive to obey to the letter God's Word as it has been revealed to them, whereas all others are rebellious. This is either because they are secularised and see no reason to try to obey, or because they have a false perception of God and his Word. Fundamentalists also seek to differentiate themselves with reference to other binary terms. They will emphasise their pure spirituality compared to the carnal depravity of the world, for example, or their scrupulous observance of ritual requirements versus the carelessness of others about such important details.

While this task of differentiation may seem demanding and tiresome to outsiders, it is highly rewarding to believers themselves. They internalise their membership into their self-concept, making their identity as believer central to their notion of who they are. Since this identity is positive, and in total contrast with the evil of others, it is important to them to maintain and enhance it. Hence differentiation indirectly motivates believers to support and fight for their fundamentalism.

But *differentiation is not enough*. To survive, fundamentalist adherents not only have to be different from everyone else. They also have to be the same as each other. They have to *conform* to the particular understanding of God's Word which their movement proclaims and the beliefs and practices which it enjoins (10). If different interpretations are held by different believers among Us, then the differences between Us and Them will become blurred and the boundary lines fuzzy. The struggle for God's truth will lose its edge. Moreover, conformity of belief is also important for survival in its own right. If a fundamentalism's survival depends upon acting decisively in the struggle against its perceived enemy, it will be hard to ensure such concerted action if the beliefs upon which it is based are not held by all its adherents. There will be disagreements about strategy and tactics, and many will not be truly committed to the actions planned. *The fundamentalisms which survive and prosper, then, are those which are not only differentiated externally but also conformist within.*

There are many ways of inducing the necessary degree of conformity in adherents. The Brethren, for example, discourage deviance by giving considerable power to the elders of each assembly. These men are chosen "by the Holy Spirit", which normally means that they are invited to join "the oversight" by its existing members. It is their task to "take aside" any deviants from orthodoxy and advise them of the error of their beliefs or actions. The next sanction is refusal of admission to the Breaking of Bread (Holy Communion), followed by "withdrawal of fellowship". However, conformity is a consequence of far more than the warnings of elders and the threat of sanctions. It is powered by two main engines. The first is an upbringing in a family of believers. The family expects attendance at worship and sets boundaries to prevent temptations even being presented, let alone succumbed to. It also guides its offspring to marry another believer. The second source of conformity is the induction of new converts into the unfamiliar environment of the movement. Any new adherent will have little idea of the beliefs and behaviour now expected of them and will take their cue from existing adherents.

Consider too the consequences of differentiation and conformity for the Haredim. These Jewish fundamentalists are clearly differentiated by their appearance and their way of life, as I have already described. They follow the teachings of specific rabbis who elucidate the requirements of the Torah regarding all areas of daily life and worship in great detail. As a consequence of both their differentiation and their conformity, the Haredim have maintained a strong influence both in Israel and in the diaspora. Because they hold the balance of power in the Knesset, they wield political power in Israel, which they exercise to maintain conservative social policies as well as to buttress their own religious interests (11). Their struggle is against less observant Jews but also against secularism and hedonism.

The second core belief, then, which assumes a cosmic conflict between God and Satan and between true believers and others, has a profound effect on the defining features and the tightly knit conformity of fundamentalisms. However, while the two core beliefs are necessary conditions for fundamentalist activity, they are not sufficient. A system of secondary beliefs is also required, which forms the material for the inspirational narratives which can motivate and justify action. Each fundamentalism has such a narrative, which, while it may follow the overall structure of the general template I outlined above, will be based on a unique belief system. While each fundamentalism is sure its secondary beliefs are correct, since they are founded on God's Word, they of course differ from the secondary beliefs of other fundamentalisms since they are based on different interpretations of that Word.

Questions for discussion

1 Are fundamentalisms unique in their emphasis on binary terms or are there other institutions, movements, or organisations which are similar in this regard? In which other respects are they similar?
2 What are likely to be the prototypes of Brethren, Taliban, and Haredi leaders, respectively? What advantages and difficulties follow from these prototypes for leaders and for followers?
3 What are the outcomes of fundamentalists' stereotyping of their enemies?
4 Why is the possession of a compelling narrative important for fundamentalist movements? What other movements find one equally important, and why?

References

1. Almond, Gabriel, Appleby, Scott, & Sivan, Emmanuel (2003) Strong Religion: The Rise of Fundamentalisms around the World. Chicago: University of Chicago Press.
2. Herriot, Peter (2020) Populism, Fundamentalism, and Identity: Fighting Talk. Cham, Switzerland: Palgrave Macmillan.
3. Lawrence, Bruce (1989) Defenders of God: The Fundamentalist Revolt Against the Modern Age. Columbia, SC: University of South Carolina Press.
4. Hostetler, John (1993) Amish Society (4th edn.) Baltimore: John Hopkins University Press.
5. Quinn, Kimberley, Macrae, Neil, & Bodenhausen, Galen (2003) Stereotyping and Impression formation: How categorical thinking shapes person perception. In Hogg, Michael & Cooper, Joel (eds.) Handbook of Social Psychology. London: Sage.
6. Naugle, David (2002) Worldview: The History of a Concept. Grand Rapids, MI: William B Eerdmans.
7. Bruce, Steve (2000) Fundamentalism. Cambridge: Polity Press.
8. Boyer, Paul (1992) When Time Shall Be No More: Prophecy Belief in Modern American Culture. Cambridge, MA: Harvard University Press.
9. Brewer, Marilynn (2009) Motivations underlying ingroup identification: Optimal distinctiveness and beyond. In Otten, Sabine, Sassenberg, Kai, & Kessler, Thomas (eds.) Intergroup Relations: The Role of Motivation and Emotion. Psychology Press: New York.

10. Martin, Robin, & Hewstone, Miles (2003) Social-influence processes of control and change: Conformity, obedience to authority, and innovation. In Hogg, Michael & Cooper, Joel (eds.) Handbook of Social Psychology. London: Sage.
11. Janner-Klausner, Laura (2016) Jewish fundamentalism. In Dunn, James (ed.) Fundamentalisms: Threats and Ideologies in the Modern World. London: IB Tauris.

Further reading

Brekke, Torkel (2012) Fundamentalism: Prophecy and Protest in an Age of Globalization. New York: Cambridge University Press.

Armstrong, Karen (2000) The Battle for God: Fundamentalism in Judaism, Christianity, and Islam. London: Harper Collins.

Herriot, Peter (2020) Populism, Fundamentalism, and Identity: Fighting Talk. Cham, Switzerland: Palgrave Macmillan.

6 Belief Systems

Why so different?

So if fundamentalisms all share the same two core beliefs, why do they differ so much from each other, to the extent that the Brethren and the Taliban, for example, are worlds apart? If we start with fundamentalists' first core belief in God's Word as the source of all truth and wisdom, then we might begin to answer this question by looking at differences between their different holy books. For ultra-orthodox Jews, the Torah and subsequent commentaries upon it constitute God's Word. The first five books of the Bible contain a great number of laws and regulations which God laid down for his people Israel. For Christians, on the other hand, the Bible implies a theology in which God's law is overlaid with his grace. Large parts of the New Testament contain detailed theological arguments to this effect. And for Muslims, the Qu'ran presents a range of injunctions regarding worship, daily life, and relations with other religions. It is therefore possible that in sincerely attempting to discern God's will in these different versions of his Word, fundamentalisms will come to different conclusions about what God wants them to do.

It is a truism that Christianity puts more emphasis on believing the right things (orthodoxy) than on doing the right things (orthopraxis), whereas for Judaism and Islam the reverse is the case. These differences do indeed reflect the differences in emphasis of their holy books. Even the exceptions can be argued to support this thesis. The Reconstructionists, for example, are Reformist Protestant fundamentalists who emphasise the importance of obeying God's law and advocate a theocracy. However, this is because they argue that the Mosaic law of the Old Testament remains the basis for the covenant between God and his people (1).

There are, however, other more persuasive explanations for the differences between fundamentalisms than the differences between their holy books. The first is the familiar issue about *interpretation*. Each fundamentalism believes that its own reading of God's Word is the only possible meaning that it can have. This follows from the proposition that

God speaks directly to believers and that the common sense reception of the Word is all that is required of them. Thus, there is no need for interpretation, since there is only one possible meaning. Of course, it turns out that one reader's common sense understanding is another's heresy, with the consequence that fundamentalisms are notoriously prone to sectarian schisms. An example from the Brethren is the split between the Open and the Exclusive factions (see p.11).

But different interpretations are only one source of division and difference. A second is the *selectivity* which fundamentalisms apply to their reading of the Word. The Word is understood to be a complete and unified expression of the nature of the Almighty himself. It would surely be considered arrogant to decide that one part of the Word is more important than another for the believer. Yet a brief look at my father's Bible indicates that selectivity is practised by the Brethren. My father's handwritten notations, which helped him when he contributed to morning worship, were far more frequent for the letters of St Paul than for other parts of the Bible. This reflects the Brethren's emphasis on the New Testament churches and their beliefs and practices (the Brethren believe themselves to be the godly remnant who faithfully put these into practice). Similarly, many fundamentalist Christians in the United States pay particular attention to those parts of the Bible that appear to relate to the apocalypse, or end times (2). And fundamentalists everywhere search out references to sexual orientation or patriarchy.

Fight or flight

Mainly as a result of interpretation and selectivity, fundamentalisms hold very different secondary beliefs. These tend to be organised into belief systems, which form the basis of each fundamentalism's key narratives. By way of illustration, there follows shortly an account of one secondary belief system, which I have labelled *"Fight or Flight"*. This binary label is misleading, since the belief system in question ranges widely across different interpretations of how God requires believers to act against his adversaries. What values should they espouse in this great struggle, and how should they express them in practice?

Values form an important component of secondary belief systems. Values are not beliefs that something is the case, or true, but rather, that some mode of conduct or end-state is preferable to its opposite (3). Examples are obedience and honesty, both of which refer to modes of conduct, and happiness and security, which are end-states or outcomes. Psychologists have proposed that the number of values is limited by the number of basic human needs, which values reflect, and that, for this reason, they are universal. The obvious differences in values between

48 Fundamentalist Beliefs

different cultures and sub-cultures may be explained in terms of different orders of priority within the same value set (4). For example, collectivist values, such as collaboration, are of greater importance in some cultures, and individualist ones, for example ambition, in others (5).

Another element of belief systems concerns *causality*. To what do we habitually attribute events and outcomes (6)? Are they the result of supernatural intervention, for example by God or Satan or Fate? Are they the outcome of human nature, or people's personalities, or habits, or emotions, or plans and intentions? Are they a consequence of specific social and cultural environments, or vast societal changes such as globalization or information technology?

As a generalisation, fundamentalists tend towards supernatural and human rather than environmental attributions. Some emphasise God's omnipotence, to the extent that he determines all events and outcomes. Others, however, consider that human agency is also at work in the world. The implications for action of this attributional difference are important. If divine omnipotence and omniscience rule alone, outcomes are determined by, and known to, God in advance. Believers therefore should accept God's will and not seek arrogantly to influence the world's course and direction. The values associated with this acceptance are likely to be such conduct values as submission and withdrawal, and end product values of humility and purity. And the likely action that follows is that of separation from the world and the drawing of tight boundaries around the enclave of believers.

If, however, attribution is to both divine and human agency, then the implications are quite different. Fundamentalists of this persuasion will conclude that they are called upon to get involved and struggle in the world on God's behalf. Their enemies will include secularism and immorality. High on their list of value priorities will be the conduct values of agency and organisation, and the ends of victory and virtue. Purity and separation are less achievable with this degree of involvement and are consequently lower in their order of priority.

Examples from Protestant and Jewish fundamentalisms will demonstrate the variety of action prompted by different positions in the Fight or Flight secondary belief system. One strand of Protestant fundamentalism asserts that God entirely determines the world's past history, present situation, and future fate (7). Past, present, and future time is divided into ages, or eras, each representing a stage in God's relationship with his chosen people and with humankind in general. The present age is the church age, in which believers eagerly await Christ's return to earth and the end days. When Christ first returns, he will take back with him into heaven all believers, an event known as "the rapture". This will leave the rest of humanity to endure various sufferings. However, God will ultimately defeat Satan and rule in perfect peace and justice, with the faithful believers doing his bidding. This particular strand of belief is termed "premillennialism", because it asserts that believers will be raptured *before* the subsequent thousand years. Another strand, however, the postmillennialists, believe that they can influence the course of history, by working to hasten the execution of God's plan. Thus, while not detracting from God's omniscience and omnipotence, they allow the possibility of human as well as supernatural agency.

The difference between these two attributions of causality may appear trivial. However, they have profound implications for other elements of the Fight or Flight belief system and for the actions to which it points. For example, premillennialists are apt to regard it as arrogant if not heretical to attempt to improve on what God has already planned. Rather, they should quietly await Christ's coming, keeping themselves pure and separate from the world, as befits the church, the bride of Christ. The only worldly contact in which they engage is the attempt to convert sinners, so that they too escape God's judgement of their sins and are raptured with Christ. Postmillennialists, on the other hand, throw themselves into the struggle against the world, with its secularism and immorality. They fight culture wars for the soul of America, fixating on issues such as abortion, sex education, and gay marriage. They use the democratic systems of their nations to achieve their ends, including election to political office, as occurred with the Moral Majority movement. They are apt to value organisation as a means, and agency and control as ends; separation and purity are further down their list of priorities. Thus, different positions taken within a secondary belief system are expressed in extremely diverse actions and indicate the importance of such systems in explaining the differences between fundamentalisms.

Another playing out of the Fight or Flight belief system can be found in the ultra-orthodox Jews, the Haredim (8). Like the premillennialists, the more traditional Haredim believe that God will determine when the Messiah comes. Their task is to study the Torah and obey it to the letter, thus building up, as it were, spiritual capital for Israel (in the sense of the Jewish people) in the eyes of God. Other fundamentalist Jews, however, believe in much more concrete interpretations. The Messiah, they believe, will lead Israel to victory in its struggle to possess the land "promised to their forefather Abraham and his seed for ever". The traditionalists do intervene in Israeli politics, but mostly to ensure two outcomes: first, the retention of their own privileges as the guardians of the nation's religious heritage, and second, as much conformity to the Torah as they can persuade the Knesset to encourage. The more recent interventionists, however, become far more involved in the political issues of the day. In particular, they concentrate on the issue of the land and its ownership and occupancy. They initiate Israeli settlements in Palestinian territory. Currently, fundamentalists occupy some of the major ministerial positions in Benjamin Netanyahu's coalition government, which depends on fundamentalist support for its survival.

If we were to ask some fundamentalists how they might respond to Part Two (chapters 4, 5, and 6), it is possible that they might not have too many arguments with chapters 4 and 5. They might agree that the two core beliefs do indeed represent vital elements of their faith. However, they would certainly not agree with much of chapter 6. There is no distinction between core and secondary beliefs, they would argue, for God's Word is a unity and has a single unchanging meaning. There is no interpretation involved on their part, for its meaning is clearly revealed. And they aren't selective, since the Word itself tells them how to read it. On the other hand, fundamentalists would agree with the psychological theory underpinning Part Two, that is, the rational relationship of beliefs and values with intentions and actions. They are convinced that it is their beliefs which compel them to act in obedience to what they think God requires of them.

Questions for discussion

1 How convincing is the distinction between core and secondary beliefs?
2 What are the top three in order of priority of your own values? Are they the top three in all situations?
3 When, if ever, do you make attributions to divine or supernatural causation? Why on these occasions? What are the consequences?
4 How do fundamentalisms choose their enemies? Why these?

References

1. Ingersoll, Julie (2015) Building God's Kingdom: Inside the World of Christian Reconstruction. New York: Oxford University Press.
2. Boyer, Paul (1992) When Time Shall Be No More: Prophecy Belief in Modern American Culture. Cambridge, MA: Harvard University Press.
3. Rokeach, Milton (1973) The Nature of Human Values. New York: Free Press.
4. Haidt, Jonathan (2013) The Righteous Mind: Why Good People are Divided by Politics and Religion. London: Penguin.
5. Triandis, Harry (2019) Individualism and Collectivism. London: Routledge.
6. Ross, Lee & Nesbitt, Richard (1991) The Person and the Situation: Perspectives of Social Psychology. New York: McGraw Hill.
7. Wojcik, Daniel (1997) The End of the World as We Know It: Faith, Fatalism, and Apocalypse in America. New York: New York University Press.
8. Lawrence, Bruce (1989) Defenders of God: The Fundamentalist Revolt Against the Modern Age. Columbia, SC: University of South Carolina Press.

Further reading

Tamney, Joseph (2002) The Resilience of Conservative Religion: The Case of Popular Conservative Protestant Congregations. Cambridge: Cambridge University Press.

Stern, Jessica (2003) Terror in the Name of God. New York: Harper Collins.

Almond, Gabriel, Appleby, Scott, & Sivan, Emmanuel (2003) Strong Religion: The Rise of Fundamentalisms around the World. Chicago: University of Chicago Press.

Part III
Motivational Foundations

7 Meaning

Identity and self

Why are people attracted and attached to fundamentalist movements? What is it that motivates believers to devote themselves to a life of separation or struggle? This is treated here as a psychological question, although of course it could be answered in theological, philosophical, political, historical, or sociological terms. In the previous chapters the classic psychological theory of reasoned action offered a coherent account of the relationship between fundamentalists' beliefs, values, and actions. There is similarly well-established psychological theory and research which relates to the question of their motivation – the theory of *identity* (1).

Given the current frequent use of the term identity in relation to social and political issues, it is necessary to outline psychological identity theory. First, a useful distinction can be drawn between personal and social identity. *Personal* identity refers to the self-concept, to the individual and unique person we think we are (2). *Social* identity, on the other hand, is our belief that we belong to a particular category of person, for example that one is a conservative, an engineer, an American, or a parent. Many such categories are combinations, for example, Black woman or British artist. Clearly, we are each likely to hold many social identities, particularly if we live in a late-modern society.

Personal identity and social identities are related, in the sense that the former is likely to incorporate the latter; part of our notion of who we are is likely to involve our political, occupational, national, and family identities, among many others. Moreover, the greater the number and variety of our social identities, the more likely our personal identity will be differentiated from that of other people (3). We will be seen as a unique and different person and will see ourselves as such.

Social identities require more than the performance of roles. Role-playing implies no more than acting in socially appropriate ways in specific situations. One may do so merely in order to comply with the norms of behaviour prevalent, for example, in one's job. Social identification, however, requires more than compliance. It involves the internalisation of the beliefs, values, and norms of the category concerned. We have to embrace its culture and allow it to become part of our self-concept, our personal identity.

Social identities serve an important function in social life. Different identities become *salient*, or uppermost, in the mind in different social situations: parent at home, for example, and employee at work. The salience of the appropriate identity will enable not only appropriate roles to be played but also the identity's beliefs and values to inform and motivate behaviour. However, situation is not the only factor which predicts which identity is salient. Social identities may also differ in terms of their centrality and *importance* to an individual's self-concept. So, notoriously, occupational identity may occupy so important a position in a person's self-concept that it dominates partner and parent identities, and work-life balance is upset. And likewise the identity of believer may so dominate the self-concept of fundamentalists that it is salient in almost every social context. The beliefs, values, and norms of their movement thus dominate the direction and motivation of their social behaviour. Every situation is part of the struggle: a birthday party or a train journey, for example, becomes an opportunity to witness.

It is the relationship between the social identity and the self-concept of fundamentalists which powers their motivation. The beliefs and values derived from their social identity differentiate them from others, and it is this difference which dominates their self-concept. Since the preservation and enhancement of the self is a powerful human motive, then the social identity of believer itself provides powerful motivation. When believers win a famous victory, fundamentalists feel victorious as individuals; and when their movement is under threat, they become less secure people. *Social and personal identities together provide the driving force for action.*

Self in the world

So how does identity's motivational power work? In the first place, it helps to satisfy the need for meaning. A fundamental need of modern humankind is to address the question "Who am I as an individual person in a social world?" To develop a self-concept, or personal identity, which makes sense of our experience and informs our social interactions is a continuing task throughout our life. It reduces our feelings of uncertainty and insecurity in our complex and constantly changing environment; and it enables us to perceive some sort of consistency in the way we conduct our lives.

The fundamentalist narrative proposes a radically simple answer to this existential question. It provides a social identity, that of believer, which is highly differentiated from other social identities. All of these latter it lumps together as "the world" or "heresy" or some other pejorative label. It requires the believer to keep this identity salient in their mind in every social situation (4). Furthermore, the fundamentalist narrative expects the social identity of believer to be the foundation of the self-concept. The self becomes *depersonalised,* to the extent that unique individuality fades into insignificance. As a result, the tricky task of reconciling the beliefs and values of the different social identities, which contribute to the self-concept of modern people, is avoided. There is only one set of beliefs and values to hold – those of the true believer.

Thus, the various conundrums which face modern humankind do not trouble believers. The second core fundamentalist belief ensures that they do not have to relate to the social world in which they live, except to shun it, convert it, or attack it. The first core belief relieves them of the task of discovering different sorts of truth, since everything has been revealed to them in God's Word. The answers to the questions which have baffled humankind for centuries have been revealed to them once and for all.

Consider first the question of *causality*. To whom or to what are we to attribute the occurrence and the consequences of the various successes and failures which individuals, groups, and societies experience (5)? Fundamentalists are quite clear. They are the outcome of the ongoing conflict between God and Satan, a conflict the ultimate outcome of which has already been determined in God's favour. The attribution is to the supernatural. When fundamentalists do make attributions to human actors, these are in effect attributions to the supernatural, since it is always God or Satan who is working through people. And attributions to abstract forces such as human nature or sin are likewise ultimately to Satan himself.

Or take the issue of *time*. How are we to understand our own past, present, and future in the context of the history of the world, its current condition, and its future prospects? Once again, fundamentalisms offer a clear and simple narrative (6). The past is dominated by a single profound event, God's revelation of his Word, a golden age indeed. However, before long Satan seduced humankind into all sorts of error and rebellion, and God's truth was treasured and obeyed only by a faithful remnant of believers. The present age is characterised by a particularly threatening assault on the faithful, and a fundamentalist resurgence is essential if they are to survive. Before long, however, God will return in glory, and his kingdom will last forever.

Finally, what are we to make of the incredible rate of *change* which the world is experiencing? The narratives which we all use to try to make sense of change are being tested to their limit. Twenty years ago, the imminence of climate catastrophe would not have featured in many such narratives. Now it is hard to imagine one in which it does not hold a dominant position. Once again, however, the fundamentalist narrative has no problems. There is only one trustworthy narrative, the truth revealed in God's Word, which is eternal and changeless. It tells us that the omnipotent God has determined history, and our task is simply to trust and obey him. In sum, fundamentalism provides clear and simple answers to complex and demanding questions and issues. This simplicity is attractive because it reduces uncertainty (7). And decreased uncertainty increases security and reduces anxiety.

Identity deployed

How, then, have fundamentalisms deployed the social identity of true believer to motivate adherents in the struggle against the enemy? The theoretical account presented in this chapter so far seems too dry and rational to explain the extraordinary zeal and energy which we perceive as characteristic. We simply cannot imagine how identity can constitute so strong a motive force and inspire such sometimes momentous action.

One of the most revealing documents regarding fundamentalist identity is the list of instructions given by Mohammed Atta, the operational director, to his fellow conspirators to prepare for the 9/11 assault on the United States (8). This demonstrates in startling detail the view of themselves and the world held by these militant Islamists. Atta frames the world situation as one of constant war – not mere conflict, but war. Following the Islamic ideologues Mawdudi and Qutb (9), he casts the parties to the conflict as the believers and the infidels, and by "infidels" is meant everyone else, even including many "heretical" Muslims.

There are two major consequences of calling this conflict "war". The first relates to the fact that *different rules* apply in war than in other human activities (10). War permits its participants to assault and kill their enemy. Hence, their "war" provides the conspirators with both the justification for the hijacking and the motivation to carry it through. The "enemy" is indeed a vast amorphous category of people, infidels or secularists, in principle everyone whom they judge not to be a true believer. Hence, these conspirators considered it their sacred duty as God's soldiers to kill a random group of air travellers. Of course, the geopolitical impact and the symbolism of the method of the assault were part of al-Qaida's strategic purpose in the minds of its leaders (11), but it is the thinking of the ordinary "soldiers" which we need to understand.

The second consequence of "war" against such an enemy is *depersonalisation*. When your target is practically everyone other than your comrades, there is no possibility of seeing anyone as an individual person. Indeed, Atta explicitly instructs his co-conspirators not to feel any anger or revenge against the airline passengers. Clearly, they are merely exemplars of a vast and nameless enemy. Moreover, depersonalisation is evident regarding *both* parties to the hijacking: Atta mentions no individual differences between the conspirators either. They are all simply comrades fighting for God against his enemies, pious Muslims who are faithful and steadfast, the jihadist vanguard. They will all win the ultimate crown of martyrdom and be welcomed among the great ones in paradise, Atta promises.

It is significant that President George W. Bush wasted no time in declaring America's "war on terror", thereby accepting the legitimacy of killing a depersonalised enemy ("terror"). In so doing, he accepted the conspirators' framing of the situation as global conflict, thereby adding to the symbolic importance of the assault. One alternative response might have been to characterise 9/11 as a criminal act of murder, to be pursued using legal and reputational sanctions.

In terms of the theory of social identity and self-concept, Atta's instructions suggest that the self-concept of the conspirators might have been starkly simple. Their dominant social identity was as God's soldiers, pious and faithful believers. It may have been so dominant as to become salient in every situation, to the exclusion of every other possible social identity, for example, son, husband or father, or even, human being. Clearly, this social identity of believer was a basic element in the self-concept. Indeed, could it have been the *only* element? There is no evidence that the conspirators were encouraged to think of themselves in any way as individuals. They may have had no personal identity. If they were thus depersonalised and only had one social identity, then that represented who they thought they were: God's soldiers.

There are some indications that this analysis can be applied to Atta himself. He rejected the possibility of marriage. He seems to have lost other social identities during the course of his radicalisation as a student. Indeed, the dedication of his postgraduate thesis on urban planning for Hamburg University reads: "My prayer and my sacrifice and my life and my death are for Allah, the Lord of the Worlds". Gratitude to his Egyptian parents or to his tutors for their support is not expressed; his entire being is by now devoted to fighting for God.

But this was no ordinary war. It was *a holy war*, and many more rules are to be followed, since the Lord of the Worlds has to be obeyed to the letter. Atta's instructions relate largely to the religious rituals which the conspirators have to complete before the time for "battle". All are derived from the Qu'ran or Sharia. They are told to read the chapters in the Qu'ran which deal with warfare. "Strike for God's sake" urges Atta. "Make sure your soul is prepared to do everything for God only". He tells them to cause as little discomfort as possible to those they are killing, as this was the Prophet's practice. On the other hand, they are to keep no prisoners alive, but rather kill them, as "no prophet should have prisoners until he has soaked the land with blood".

The rituals which the conspirators are instructed to perform are essentially rituals of purification. They had to shave their body hair, shower, and apply cologne before they boarded the plane. They had to be ritually pure because they were going to be sacrificial martyrs. "Purify your soul from all unclean things", Atta urges, "completely forget something called "this world". They will be using faith and knives, the same spiritual weapons as used in the golden age of the Prophet, whereas the "enemy" will use modern technology. And then, a final call for fortitude and obedience: "… every one of you should prepare to carry out his role in a way that would satisfy God. You should clench your teeth, as the pious early generations did……sing songs to boost morale, as the pious first generations did in the throes of battle, to bring calm tranquillity and joy to the hearts of his brothers".

So the hijackers had a single view of the world and their place and purpose within it. They had complete certainty about who they were and what they should do. They were soldiers of God, and their task was to attack and kill his enemies. And so, joyfully, off they flew to martyrdom and their place in paradise.

Questions for discussion

1 Do you habitually draw the distinction between personal identity and social identity? Why have both become such prominent ideas in social and political discussions?
2 Can you think of situations where someone had an inappropriate social identity salient in their mind? How did they act? What were the consequences?
3 Why are simple explanations attractive to people? And why, in the first place, are we so eager to explain?
4 How did radical Islamists succeed in radicalising young men to commit mass murder?

References

1. Hogg, Michael, & Abrams, Dominic (2003) Intergroup behaviour and social identity. In Hogg, Michael, & Cooper, Joel (eds.) Handbook of Social Psychology. London: Sage.
2. Baumeister, Roy, & Bushman, Brad (2011) The Self: Social Psychology and Human Nature (2nd edn.) Belmont, CA: Cengage Learning.
3. Brewer, Marilynn, & Caporael, Linnda (2006) Social identity motives in evolutionary perspective. In Brown, Rupert, & Capozza, Dora (eds.) Social Identities: Motivational, Emotional, and Cultural Influences. Hove: Psychology Press.

4. Tajfel, Henri & Turner, John (1986) The social identity theory of intergroup behaviour. In Worchel, Stephen, & Austin, William (eds.) Psychology of Intergroup Relations. Chicago: Nelson Hall.
 5. Ross, Lee & Nisbett, Richard (1991) The Person and the Situation: Perspectives of Social Psychology. New York: McGraw-Hill.
 6. Hall, John (2009) Apocalypse: From Antiquity to the Empire of Modernity. Cambridge: Polity Press.
 7. Hogg, Michael & Mullen, Barbara (1999) Joining groups to reduce uncertainty: Subjective uncertainty reduction and group identification. In Abrams, Dominic & Hogg, Michael (eds.) Social Identity and Social Cognition. Oxford: Blackwell.
 8. Herriot, Peter (2007) Religious Fundamentalism and Social Identity. London: Routledge.
 9. Qutb, Sayyid (1981) Milestones. New Delhi: Markazi Maktaba Islami.
10. Juergensmeyer, Mark (2000) Terror in the Mind of God: The Global Rise of Religious Violence. Berkeley, CA: University of California Press.
11. Gerges, Fawaz (2005) The Far Enemy: Why Jihad Went Global. New York: Cambridge University Press.

Further reading

Jenkins, Richard (2008) Social Identity (3rd edn.) London: Routledge.
Herriot, Peter (2007) Religious Fundamentalism and Social Identity. London: Routledge.
Juergensmeyer, Mark (2000) Terror in the Mind of God: The Global Rise of Religious Violence. Berkeley, CA: University of California Press.

8 Agency

Social agency

A decreasing sense of agency characterises today's world. Many feel that their lives are being controlled by forces which they don't understand and feel unable to resist. For example, the growth of artificial intelligence and its unregulated development currently makes people uneasy and open to offers to recover a degree of control over their lives.

One of the results of this feeling of powerlessness is the huge popularity enjoyed at present by the self-help industry, especially in Western late-modern societies which place a high value on individualism. Its practitioners claim that it can enable people to achieve their potential to become the people they want to become. Its aim is therefore to help individuals to develop their personal identity. And its practitioners' recommendations generally take the form of urging their clients to work hard on improving their self (1). The developed self is the product of following the instructions of their guide as they undertake this demanding task, which clearly requires a high degree of self-consciousness and self-awareness. To feel they have achieved it must surely make the clients confident that they have impacted successfully their lives and their futures. They feel a sense of *personal agency*.

Fundamentalists too can attribute events and their outcomes to themselves. Their explanation, however, is not in terms of their own personal development and uniqueness upon which they have worked so hard. Rather, it is their *social identity* as believers which enables them to claim responsibility for successes. "*We* won the victory", they can claim, regardless of the fact that they personally may not have been involved in the particular struggle in question. A victory for some is a victory for us all. And anyway, those who were involved of course attribute the victory to the Almighty. Their own part was simply to obey God's will as best as they could, acting as his agents. But it was God who willed it, conquering his enemies and Satan himself. The 9/11 conspirators obeyed God's commands, and he permitted them to join the glorious company of martyrs.

Now in terms of aims and objectives, 9/11 seemed at the time, both to militant Islamists and to the rest of the world, to have been a success. There are certain other fundamentalist victories which also are hard to deny. Iran and Afghanistan, for example, remain under theocratic rule at time of writing. During Trump's presidency, various fundamentalist luminaries had extensive access to his ear, and used it to urge, among other things, the repeal of the Supreme Court's historic Roe vs Wade ruling establishing the right to abortion. More generally, fundamentalist movements have flourished in those nations where nationalist populist politicians have gained power, for example, India, Brazil, and Israel. In all these cases, all the adherents of the movement concerned could feel a sense of agency, since "we" had succeeded.

These were all instances where success was generally understood to have been achieved, for example, in terms of political influence, media visibility, and social change. Not only fundamentalists themselves but also "the world" thought the fundamentalists had won victories in terms of achieving meaningful objectives. There are many other criteria for success available to fundamentalists, however, which are certainly not based on worldly, but rather on spiritual values. No one else might consider a victory to have been won, but so long as fundamentalists themselves believe their actions to have been a success, they can consider themselves to have been responsible and experience a sense of agency.

Consider, for example, the value of *purity*. Fundamentalists talk about purity in several contexts. Sometimes the reference is a general one, where the temptations of "the world" are successfully resisted. A more specific instance is sexual purity, which carries immense importance and is a powerful target for Satan's wiles. And purity of doctrine is defended with zeal, since fundamentalists are the faithful remnant who have preserved it as it was in the golden age of the faith. To have successfully defended purity, then, is likely to enhance their feelings of agency, even though some of the outcomes might be regarded by "the world" as constituting miserable failure.

Purity of doctrine

The Calvinist faction in the Church of England provides a good example of such an attempt to defend purity. As one might expect of a Protestant fundamentalism, its concern is primarily with orthodoxy, the purity of doctrine. It represents itself as being the minority fighting for the historic truth of the Reformation as represented by Calvin, that is, *sola scriptura* (by scripture alone). In other words, Calvin was asserting that the Bible and not the Church, nor Christian experience, nor human reason, is the sole source of doctrinal authority (the first core belief of fundamentalism).

After the English Reformation, repeated bloody conflicts between Reformers and Catholics finally ceased being bloody, and were replaced by the Anglican Church of England (2). Since its function was to unify the warring parties, and as the national established church representing the nation as a whole, the Church of England had of necessity to be a "broad church", containing and tolerating a range of beliefs and practices. As an institution, it adapted to societal change, in particular to the industrial revolution and the consequent movement away from rural parishes to the cities. And it accommodated itself to, and indeed sometimes led, social improvements such as the abolition of slavery and child labour (3).

The radical social changes which occurred in the three decades after the Second World War were, however, particularly challenging. Specifically, changing attitudes regarding gender roles and sexual orientation presented major problems for a church which was, like other denominations, patriarchal in its beliefs, values, structures, and practices. It was not surprising, then, that minorities who had historically suffered discrimination regarded the Church as an institution which was continuing to deny them equal rights. Their advocacy groups supported women in their quest to be ordained as priests. The Church's Synod, consisting of bishops, clergy, and lay members, for its part voted for the ordination of women in 1992. This was the cue for a long and continuing struggle within the Church on a sequence of issues: gay Christians, gay priests, gay bishops, women bishops, and gay blessings (4). These were resolved in favour of the minorities concerned, but only after prolonged conflict, and long after public opinion had itself shifted decisively (attitudes towards LGBT issues have shown the greatest change of any area in the previous 40 years of the British Social Attitude Surveys). The consequence was that the Church was perceived increasingly as misogynistic and homophobic, particularly by the young for whom these issues were especially important.

The Calvinist fundamentalists who fomented these struggles represent a powerful minority within the Church. They have the advantage of being a movement rather than an institution, and so are able to concentrate on their few chosen issues. They are extremely well organised, with wealthy congregations, able and media-savvy leaders, single issue pressure groups, and university Christian Unions and theological colleges all collaborating (5). They have excelled in ecclesiastical politics and media coverage. Their single-issue campaigning organisations, for example, are named Anglican Mainstream, Reform, and Anglican Mission in England. These names are deliberately chosen to challenge the authority of the Church of England. The Calvinists call themselves mainstream, whereas they are in fact a minority in the Church. They claim for themselves the legacy of the Reformation. And they imply that they, together with other members of the Anglican Communion, are called to act as missionaries to the corrupt and secularised established Church. They immediately provide a media response to events such as the expulsion from her professional body of a psychotherapist who practised conversion therapy on gay people. In sum, they devote much of their time and energy to defending fundamentalist positions which they believe to be orthodox biblical doctrine.

Thus, the Anglican Calvinists represent themselves as the faithful remnant fighting for the orthodox faith of their fathers, a minority persecuted by a secularised bureaucracy. They have threatened to leave the Church, extracting various concessions which permit them to remain pure and unsullied by contact with those with whom they cannot in principle have fellowship. So, for example, they can be ministered to by so-called "flying bishops", who, like them, do not approve of women bishops or gay priests or whatever the current issue is. Their overall attitude to the denomination to which they belong is summed up by one of their most prominent leaders, Paul Perkin, as a worldly church – a church that is of the world, that is infected by the world, that is unbelieving like the world, that is immoral as the world, that is not very present in the world, and is running away from the world.

Clearly, this particular fundamentalist movement is extremely effective at inflicting a constant and draining conflict on its own denomination. It does so in the name of purity and conformity of doctrine, contrasted with the more varied beliefs and practices of the "broad church" which graciously continues to treat it as fellow Anglicans. While it has not succeeded in reversing the Church's progress towards liberalisation, it has certainly managed to slow it down and to divert the Church's resources and energies to internal issues and away from its societal mission. In sum, it has every justification in feeling that it has exercised considerable agency in defence of supposed doctrinal purity.

Obedience as agency

However, it's not necessary to fight the secular enemy without, or the apostate enemy within, to feel a sense of agency. It's enough to simply obey God's Word and do his will, even when conflict with others is not involved. We believers can conquer Satan in our own lives, resist temptation, and fulfil all the requirements of God's law. And we don't achieve these results as individuals, but as the faithful few, determined to maintain together the rituals and practices that he requires of us.

So, for example, the Brethren treat as their two most important obligations to the Almighty the celebration of the Lord's Supper (Holy Communion), and the preaching of the gospel so that sinners may be saved (6). These they operationalise in terms of the weekly breaking of bread by believers, and the Gospel Service aimed at the conversion of sinners. Even though the results of their obedience are not apparent, they can feel that they are faithfully fulfilling God's will by continuing to hold these services. Similarly, the male Haredim may spend their entire lives studying the Torah and obeying its rigorous ritual requirements in extraordinary detail. The benefits are construed in a spiritual sense as preparing God's people for the coming of the Messiah (7). And the Taliban are concerned to enforce observance of Sharia law in the theocracy that is Afghanistan. They are acting in their view as God's agents, ensuring the obedience which he requires.

It is not hard to see why the sense of agency provided by fundamentalisms should be so important and attractive to their adherents. The world appears to be changing at an ever-increasing rate, and furthermore, nobody appears to be in control of this process. Vast impersonal forces such as climate crisis, pandemics, inequalities, technology, and globalisation determine our outcomes, we feel, not we ourselves or our democratic institutions. In such a worldview, fundamentalist belief provides the ideal alternative. Instead of change, it provides an eternal and unchanging constant: God's Word and his Law. And instead of helplessness, alienation, and despair, it gives adherents the opportunity to act as God's agents to help him bring about his victorious kingdom and rule.

Questions for discussion

1 Why are self-help programs so popular? What are their advantages and disadvantages to their followers and to societies?
2 What are the advantages and disadvantages of social identification? Compare and contrast self-help and fundamentalism in this respect.
3 Why is purity so important a value to fundamentalists? What is its particular relevance to their social identity as believers?
4 What is rewarding about paying constant attention to the detailed requirements of God's law?

References

1. Bauman, Zygmunt (1998) Globalization: The Human Consequences. Cambridge: Polity Press.
2. MacCulloch, Diarmuid (2003) The Reformation: A History. New York: Viking.
3. Furlong, Monica (2000) C of E: The State It's In. London: Hodder & Stoughton.
4. Bates, Stephen (2004) A Church at War: Anglicans and Homosexuality. London: IB Tauris.

5. Herriot, Peter (2016) Warfare and Waves: Calvinists and Charismatics in the Church of England. Eugene, OR: Wipf & Stock.
6. Herriot, Peter (2018) The Open Brethren: A Christian Sect in the Modern World. Cham, Switzerland: Palgrave Macmillan.
7. Kress, Michael (2012) The State of Orthodox Judaism Today. Jewish Virtual Library www.jewishvirtuallibrary.org.

Further reading

Herriot, Peter (2020) Populism, Fundamentalism, and Identity: Fighting Talk. Cham, Switzerland: Palgrave Macmillan.

Davie, Grace (2015) Religion in Britain: A Persistent Paradox (2nd edn.) Chichester: Wiley-Blackwell.

Bates, Stephen (2004) A Church at War: Anglicans and Homosexuality. London: I.B. Tauris.

9 Self-esteem

Association and comparison

The maintenance and enhancement of the self is a primary source of human reward and motivation, once basic survival needs have been met (1). For many modern people with a highly *personal* and individualised self-concept, self-development is their primary motivation and reward. For fundamentalists, however, their self-concept is centred on their *social* identity as believers, and it is this which is the source of their self-esteem. Self-esteem can be defined as one's attitude towards one's self, negative (low) or positive (high) (2) and is derived for fundamentalists directly from their social identity.

How does this happen? First and foremost, fundamentalists derive high self-esteem from their *two core beliefs* and the values associated with them. First, God has spoken to them through his Word, and they have obeyed him; and second, a cosmic war is being fought between God and Satan, and they alone are on God's side. These two beliefs offer several good reasons for increased self-esteem. For example, it is we (and therefore I myself) to whom God has spoken. We have listened to him and obeyed his commands, staying faithful and pure as we follow the prototypical example of the righteous few. We have conformed to the pattern of worship and of life that he has ordained. And we have steadfastly opposed his enemy, the secular world with its polluted morality.

So, there are two pathways to high fundamentalist self-esteem. The first is by *their association* with God himself, who is by definition omnipotent, omniscient, and holy. And the second is by *favourable comparison* (3) of themselves, faithful and pure, with God's enemies, who are stereotyped as *un*faithful and *im*pure. The believers themselves are totally differentiated from these enemies. They are the faithful few, conforming to the same true beliefs, right values, and holy practices, while the world is completely deceived by Satan into false beliefs, wrong values, and immoral practices. It is not difficult to emerge with a high level of self-esteem when the contrast is as starkly drawn as this.

DOI: 10.4324/9781003471981-13

History, causality, norms, and roles

The various fundamentalist *secondary belief systems*, which derive from the two core beliefs, provide many more grounds for high self-esteem. The account of *human history*, for example, assigns them the role of historic guardians of the original revelation of God to humankind (through Moses, Christ, or Mohammed). The present crisis characterises them as fighting for the very survival of the faith in a time of existential threat. And in the future reign of God on earth, they will be given positions of authority in his kingdom. What is more, God has revealed these truths to them alone as his privileged followers. With roles such as these, who could fail to recognise their own importance on the broad canvas of human history?

Another secondary belief system related to self-esteem concerns *causality*. Fundamentalists typically attribute events and outcomes to supernatural causes: God or Satan. However, they consider themselves to be obedient agents of God, carrying out his will in the world. As I argued in the previous chapter, this provides a strong sense of agency – they can work wonders for God if they trust and obey him. Again, association with the Almighty and his omnipotence must surely contribute to a high level of self-esteem. This agency is typically exercised in alternative ways: flight or fight, for example. Whichever of these directions is taken, it enables believers to practice the divinely approved virtues of purity, humility, and submission, or bravery, fortitude, and sacrifice.

Other sources of self-esteem derive from correctly following the *norms and practices* characteristic of fundamentalisms. For example, a high proportion of fundamentalist adherents are brought up in fundamentalist families. The patriarchal family is therefore likely to have been their experience and model. If they are converts later in life, on the other hand, patriarchal family arrangements are likely to be insisted upon by the movement if they are not in place already. The result is often a degree of self-satisfaction with one's success at obeying God's supposed template for the family, with well-defined roles as the authoritative husband, the submissive wife, and pious parents bringing up their children to become believers. Again, favourable comparison with "the world" brings added self-esteem, given the fluidity of the modern family.

A related source of self-esteem is the social acceptance and *approval of fellow believers*. This is likely to be highly rewarding, since we like people who are similar to ourselves (4), and fundamentalisms are populated by conformists who believe, value, and do the same things as each other. They are also united against a common enemy. Moreover, a fundamentalist group or organisation offers a wide variety of roles necessary to ensure its survival and growth and to carry out the ritual requirements of the faith. Adherents can find roles which are valued, and to which their capabilities are suited, thus experiencing the approval of others and the satisfaction of a job done well. As the Psalm has it, "I had rather be a doorkeeper in the house of my God than to dwell in the tents of wickedness" (Psalm 84 v. 10).

Defence mechanisms

Neither this chapter nor the two preceding ones are intended to reduce fundamentalist religious experience merely to the meeting of psychological needs for meaning, agency, and self-esteem. Rather, I have taken one among many possible perspectives, based in this case on psychological theories of motivation which apply to people in modern societies in general. Fundamentalists do not have different psychological needs to everyone else. What does make them relatively unusual, however, is that they put all their motivational eggs into one basket. Most modern people have a range of different opportunities to meet these needs. They may do so through their personal identity as a unique individual. They may also have several social identities, each of which can potentially meet them to a degree: their occupational or family or local identities, for example.

Fundamentalists, on the other hand, depend largely on their social identity as believers in meeting their psychological needs, an identity which constitutes their self-concept as a whole. Hence the survival and, preferably, success of their fundamentalism are necessary for their own psychological survival. This is why they are so willing to explain away what others regard as obvious failures or inconsistencies (5). The classic example is described in *"When Prophecy Fails"* (6), which details how American Protestant fundamentalists explained the failure of Christ to return on the appointed day in terms of their own misinterpretation of Biblical prophecy. Or consider the case of the snake-handling sect, the Church of God, operating mainly in West Virginia (7). These fundamentalists took literally the words of St Mark's Gospel, ch 16 v.18 and believed they could pick up venomous snakes and not be harmed. When the handler was not bitten, the scripture was fulfilled; but when the inevitable happened, this was attributed to the handler's sin, for example, of pride.

However, most fundamentalist explanations are less self-critical. Frequently, events which others describe as failures are reinterpreted as successes. All criticisms and attacks are treated as proof that they must be keeping the faith, since persecution is the proof of faithfulness and a badge of honour. Some enemies may have such a low estimation of them as to ridicule them. Others may be afraid of them enough to seek to destroy them. But either way, they can experience a high level of self-esteem, for such opposition must mean that they are fighting well for God, since Satan is treating them as his enemy.

Trump's courtiers

Of course, those fundamentalisms which prefer strategies of fight and engagement to those of flight and withdrawal are more likely to gain the psychological rewards of agency and self-esteem. Nowhere has this been more evident than in fundamentalists' engagement with President Trump (8). Trump realised early in his campaign for the presidency that Evangelical Christians in general, and fundamentalists in particular, were an essential constituency to be won over if he was to win the election. He therefore revived the practices of the 1970s, when the Moral Majority, led by such luminaries as Jerry Falwell and Pat Robertson, achieved considerable political influence (9). They had gained national support by representing America as a Christian nation, a shining city on a hill, threatened by the increasing tide of secularism and immorality. The issues they focussed on were, for various different historical reasons, abortion, the appointment of Supreme Court judges, and relations with the state of Israel, along with other disputes in the so-called culture wars.

Trump encouraged fundamentalist leaders to visit him at the White House and take part in various well-publicised events. This enabled them to represent themselves as having access and influence at the national level. They included Jerry Falwell Jr and Franklin Graham, who had inherited their famous fathers' ministries. Neither they nor Trump saw any good reason to change the issues on which the previous generation of fundamentalist leaders had campaigned. However, there was one difficulty they faced in justifying this situation to their adherents: Trump himself. He was, to put it mildly, hardly a paragon of obedience to God's Word.

This elephant in the room was quickly neutered. The Trump narrative was updated to include a very recent experience of repentance of sin and conversion to a new-found faith in the saving work of Christ. Indeed, one of the influential fundamentalist leaders claimed to have been present to help him to embrace salvation. At a stroke, this narrative update explained and excused his sins. The more egregious his sinful behaviour, the better he fitted into the classic stereotype of the notorious sinner saved by grace, and the more explicable was his continuing bad behaviour. Someone who had sunk so low would not quickly manage to learn the new ways of righteousness and holiness.

Other supposedly Biblically sound reasons were adduced to justify fundamentalist leaders in their courtship of Trump. He was likened to rulers described in the Old Testament who benefited the Jews, although they themselves were gentiles. Rulers may not be fully practising believers, but the Almighty nevertheless chooses them to support his purposes for his people. Moreover, it was clear that there was a conspiracy to blacken Trump's reputation by various secret and powerful global elites, who did not want him to Make America Great Again.

Having dealt with the character problem to the satisfaction of their adherents, fundamentalist leaders felt able to claim that it was their access and influence which persuaded Trump to take forward their policy agenda. Federal law regarding abortion was fundamentally changed by the repeal of the Wade v Roe ruling in favour of the right to abortion, leaving it to individual states' legislatures to rule on the issue. This was made possible by Trump's choice of conservative Supreme Court judges whenever vacancies became available. Moreover, in accord with fundamentalist eschatological beliefs regarding Israel and the Jews, Trump transferred the American embassy to the holy city of Jerusalem. He also supported the nationalist government of Benjamin Netanyahu, propped up by ultra-orthodox political parties.

So in terms of influence over policy, fundamentalist leaders could claim more success than the previous generation. But the resulting increased sense of agency and higher self-esteem was not limited to them. Since adherents identify so strongly with the movement, their leaders' access and influence reflected well on them too. It was us Trump was listening to, they were convinced, not just the leadership.

In sum, the simplicities of the fundamentalist identity nevertheless meet the psychological needs for meaning, agency, and self-esteem which the institutions of modern societies are finding it increasingly difficult to satisfy.

Questions for discussion

1 Why is self-esteem currently considered so important for individual well-being? What are the likely personal and social consequences of this emphasis?
2 What advantages and disadvantages does fundamentalism have compared with other social movements in terms of its appeal to self-esteem?
3 Given their skill at explaining away failure, what sort of evidence, if any, might persuade a believer of the reality?
4 Who was playing whom – Trump, or the courtiers?

References

1. Maslow, Abraham (2022) A Theory of Human Motivation. Floyd, VA: Wilder Publications.
2. Sedikides, Constantine & Gregg, Aiden (2003) Portraits of the Self. In Hogg, Michael & Cooper, Joel (eds.) Handbook of Social Psychology. London: Sage
3. Collins, Richard (1996) For better for worse: The impact of upward social comparison on self-evaluation. *Psychological Bulletin*, 119, 51–69.

4. Byrne, Donn (1971) The Attraction Paradigm. New York: Academic Press.
5. Schimmel, Solomon (2012) The Tenacity of Unreasonable Beliefs: Fundamentalism and the Fear of Truth. New York: Oxford University Press.
6. Festinger, Leon, Riecken, Henry, & Schachter, Henry (1956) When Prophecy Fails. New York: Harper Collins.
7. Hood, Ralph, Hill, Peter, & Williamson, Paul (2005) The Psychology of Religious Fundamentalism. New York: Guilford.
8. Fea, John (2018) Believe Me: The Evangelical Road to Donald Trump. Grand Rapids, MI: Eerdmans.
9. Carpenter, Joel (1997) Revive Us Again: The Reawakening of American Fundamentalism. New York: Oxford University Press.

Further reading

Lienesch, Michael (1993) Redeeming America: Piety and Politics in the New Christian Right. Chapel Hill, NC: University of North Carolina Press.

Fea, John (2018) Believe Me: The Evangelical Road to Donald Trump. Grand Rapids, MI: Eerdmans.

Schimmel, Solomon (2012) The Tenacity of Unreasonable Beliefs: Fundamentalism and the Fear of Truth. New York: Oxford University Press.

Part IV
Social Foundations

10 Leadership

Leader as prototype

How, then, do fundamentalisms actually work, not so much in the minds of adherents, but rather on the ground as social systems? The first explanation which occurs to many is in terms of the concept of leadership. It must, we imagine, have taken amazing powers of persuasion to induce modern people to commit to such counter-cultural ideas and activities.

The leader or leaders of most social institutions, movements, and organisations attract considerable attention and achieve high visibility. As a result, inspirational influence is typically attributed to them, and they are generally supposed to be responsible for the strategic direction taken and the cultural beliefs, values, and norms which dominate. Fundamentalisms are no different from other social systems in this respect. Fundamentalist leaders too are credited with power and influence, both by adherents and by observers. They are also frequently credited with some added charismatic quality.

Leaders in general have historically been defined in terms of a set of personal qualities all of which they possess. A popular examination question used to be "Leaders are born, not made": Discuss. Followers were, by default, those who did not possess these qualities. More recently, leadership discussion has concentrated more on the relationship between leaders and followers, with their mutual expectations as to their respective roles an important and negotiated element of that relationship. Today, then, greater emphasis is placed by commentators and scholars on the social process of leadership than on the character of leaders. Moreover, it is now recognised that the role of leader can be exercised by different people in different situations and by people at different levels of the organisation or movement.

Further, the practice of leadership seems to have changed recently, in line with the increasing importance of communication and digital media. Instead of leaders with professional, organisational, and political

DOI: 10.4324/9781003471981-15

knowledge and skills, a much more symbolic and performative form of leadership has become valued. The essential requirement now is to personify and act out the social identity of one's supporters. The successful leader has to at least pretend to be one of Us, embodying the beliefs and values and norms of his or her constituency. Since that constituency is frequently defined by its enemies, the leader is above all on our side, standing up for Us against Them. Both populist governments and religious fundamentalisms are based on the maintenance of a constant struggle between Us and Them (1), with the social identity of Us being highlighted by the contrast with Them (2). Trump, Orban, Netanyahu, Erdogan, Abascal, and Modi are current political leaders who foster such culture wars and cultivate fundamentalists as allies.

However, the two most important tasks of leaders remain, as they have always been, first, *to meet the psychological needs of their followers*; and, second, *to initiate strategic change*. Fundamentalist leaders are no different to other leaders regarding the first of these tasks. They need, first, to ensure that adherents embrace a worldview and self-concept which provide them with clear meaning in a chaotic world; to provide a sense of agency which relieves their feelings of helplessness and alienation; and to enhance their self-esteem, diminished by their present loss of social status and value. Increased meaning, agency, and self-esteem go a long way towards satisfying psychological needs.

How, then, do fundamentalist leaders set about this demanding task? Their primary requirement is to provide for followers a prototype of what it means to be a believer (3). This is a model of the ideal believer, and the ideal is derived from the two core beliefs and their associated values. Thus, the prototypical believer obeys God's Word and struggles with God's enemies. He or she values holiness and hates sin. The successful fundamentalist leader embodies and performs this prototype on as large a stage as he can command. Osama bin Laden certainly commanded a global stage, but still took care to maintain his reputation as a holy and ascetic man of God (4).

Believers identify with the movement, and the movement is personified and embodied in its leader. Hence, believers identify with their leader, and he acquires authority and commands loyalty. If he continues to maintain the prototype consistently by his words and actions, he will build up enough trust and credit to be able to address the second major leadership task he faces – to change the movement's strategic direction in the light of its changing context (5). Given the fundamentalist emphasis on the unchanging nature of true belief and practice, this is no easy task. It is far easier for the leader simply to continue to maintain and enhance his prototypicality. Many sects have disappeared because their leaders failed to adapt their strategic thinking in the light of social, political, or economic change.

Balancing acts

The balancing act that fundamentalist leaders have to perform, then, is a tricky one. They have to be obedient servants of the eternal God, keeping his commandments to the letter and visibly performing their prototypical role; but at the same time, they have to be prepared to act differently if the movement needs to change its strategy and tactics in order to survive and prosper. The best-known classical proponent of this balancing act was Jerry Falwell senior, the fundamentalist American Protestant (6). By the 1980s, he had built up sufficient credit throughout his prototypical separatist career to lead a basic strategic revolution among Fundamentalists. He persuaded them to break with tradition and collaborate with Evangelicals and Charismatics in a coalition to engage in a political battle with godless secularism. Other Protestants were now no longer heretics, the enemy within; and not all politicians were the enemy without, the sinful world. America could once again become a Christian nation under God, and Falwell and his allies had succeeded in leading a major strategic change of direction.

However, there are more recent and more ambiguous examples available. Many have found 21st century leadership too demanding a challenge. Modern fundamentalist movements and organisations often do not have a single officially appointed leader. Rather, leaders exercise personal influence through media and political challenge. A good example is the Orthodox Jew, Rabbi Dov Lipman, a politician, author, television and press pundit, and religious teacher and luminary. The context is the nature of the relationship between the Haredim and the State of Israel (7). Historically the Haredim had been excused military service and had been educated in entirely religious schools and colleges so that they had little to offer by way of occupational benefit to the nation. They themselves argued that their value was in acting as the spiritual few who were hastening the Messiah's arrival by their study of the Torah and their pious observance, thus saving not only the nation but the world. Lipman realised that this state of affairs could not continue, as the Haredim's privileged position was supported by an ever-decreasing number of both religious and secular Israelis.

Elected to the Knesset in 2013, Lipman campaigned for a universal requirement of some form of national service; a secular component in all schools which received government support; Orthodox synagogues being made available for worship by other Jews; and recognition of the support of "Righteous Gentiles" (those who supported Israel). These measures would, Lipman believed, enable the Haredim to continue to flourish and play a role in Israeli society. He was, however, overtaken by two circumstances. The first was the overwhelming counter-influence of militants illegally annexing Palestinian territory by planting settlements, to the extent that they occupied important cabinet positions in Netanyahu's 2022 coalition government. Lipman was advocating a more moderate position of adjustment, out of tune with the increasingly polarised trend of Israeli politics. The second reason for Lipman's loss of influence was the classic one of failing to maintain the standards of the Haredim prototype. In 2014, he was first accused of sexual harassment, and in 2021 he lost his position as secretary general of the World Confederation of United Zionists.

Distributed leadership

It is now a truism that leadership is not exercised only by those officially recognised as the leaders of a movement. Leaders are found, and leadership is exercised, at every level. I considered movement leadership from a social scientific perspective in the previous section. However, local groups of fundamentalist adherents base their decisions about whom to follow and what authority to bestow on him, as ever, on their beliefs. For example, their belief system draws a sharp distinction between the spiritual and the carnal, God and Man. It is God's decisions which matter, not Man's.

The Brethren's appointment of elders in the local assembly is a case in point (8). It is God, through his Holy Spirit, who develops a Brother to be an elder, and calls him when he is ready for that responsibility. And it is the Spirit again who inspires the existing elders to recognise that he (the Spirit) has worked in the life of the Brother in question to bring him to this point. From a "worldly" perspective, this process might be construed as a self-perpetuating oligarchy, or even a gerontocracy, destined to result in the inevitable decline of the assembly. But for the Brethren, it represents obedience to God's Word about church order. Any idea that human decision-making is involved, let alone that the members should be consulted, is out of the question.

The same emphasis on obedience to God's Word underpins the ubiquitous attribution of leadership and headship to male believers and followership and submission to female ones. Some readers may have reacted unfavourably to my use of the masculine pronoun in the previous paragraphs. However, it is factually correct, since every fundamentalist movement is sexist. From a "worldly" point of view, this is hardly surprising, for fundamentalists believe that their religion's holy book is God's Word to them personally. These holy books were written by people who lived in patriarchal societies and allocated religious and social roles strictly according to gender. Hence modern believers are convinced that God has commanded them to follow pre-modern patriarchal beliefs and practices. Moreover, many fundamentalisms hold Western liberal democracies to be decadent bastions of godless secularism, evidenced in many ways but in particular in the increasing power and influence of women.

Male dominance is exercised in a variety of ways. The Brethren, for example, require women not to contribute as speakers in services, except where only women are present. They also expect wives to submit to the authority of their husbands in family matters and to play traditional female homebuilding and family rearing roles. If a Sister steps out of line, her husband is expected to reprove her and set her straight. The Taliban, on the other hand, go round publicly beating women whom they find making some mistake in the Islamic dress code and (occasionally) executing them for engaging in sexual activity outside marriage (9). Yet despite the obvious difference in severity of sanctions, it is the same belief in patriarchy that Brethren and Taliban both hold. There are several similarities between all fundamentalisms which symbolise this male dominance. All, for example, expect women to cover their heads, in public or at worship or both (covering the head signifies submission to authority). All blame women for the sin of Eve the temptress, arousing the passions of unfortunate men helpless to resist a glimpse of the slightest part of the female body.

However, the most important overall theme of this chapter is the extraordinary success of fundamentalist leaders in satisfying adherents' overwhelming need for meaning in a changing world. Their strategies are the inevitable outcome of their two core beliefs, which are a reaction against secular modernity. But the result is an absolutely clear differentiation between fundamentalism and other social movements. To become an adherent of such a counter-cultural movement may consequently be a big ask. But the social identity and the associated struggle which follow give meaning and purpose to many lives. They also generate levels of motivation and loyalty which are the envy of leaders in many other social systems.

Questions for discussion

1 Think of a leader whom you have followed. Why do you think you followed them? If you stopped being a follower, why was this?
2 What other motivations in addition to obedience to God's Word might explain fundamentalism's universal norm of male power and authority?
3 What if anything differentiates fundamentalist leaders from populist ones?

References

1. Mudde, Cas & Kaltwasser, Cristobal (2017) Populism: A Very Short Introduction. New York: Oxford University Press.

2. Herriot, Peter (2020) Populism, Fundamentalism, and Identity: Fighting Talk. Cham, Switzerland: Palgrave Macmillan.
3. Haslam, Alexander, Reicher, Stephen, & Platow, Michael (2011) The New Psychology of Leadership, Identity, Influence, and Power. Hove: Psychology Press.
4. Gerges, Fawaz (2005) The Far Enemy: Why Jihad Went Global. New York: Cambridge University Press.
5. Lienesch, Michael (1993) Redeeming America: Piety and Politics in the New Christian Right. Chapel Hill, NC: University of North Carolina Press.
6. Harding, Susan (2000) The Book of Jerry Falwell: Fundamentalist Language and Politics. Princeton: Princeton University Press.
7. Janner-Klausner, Laura (2016) Jewish Fundamentalism. In Dunn, James (ed.) Fundamentalisms: Threats and Ideologies in the Modern World. London: IB Tauris.
8. Herriot, Peter (2018) The Open Brethren: A Christian Sect in the Modern World. Cham, Switzerland: Palgrave Macmillan.
9. Silinsky, Mark (2014) The Taliban: Afghanistan's Most Lethal Insurgents. New York: Barnes & Noble.

Further reading

Haslam, Alexander, Reicher, Stephen, & Platow, Michael (2011) The New Psychology of Leadership, Identity, Influence, and Power. Hove: Psychology Press.

Bruce, Steve (1996) Religion in the Modern World: From Cathedrals to Cults. Oxford: Oxford University Press.

Watt, David (2002) Bible-Carrying Christians: Conservative Protestants and Social Power. New York: Oxford University Press.

11 Conformity

Benefits of conformity

Fundamentalist leaders, then, act out and personify the prototype of the ideal adherent of their movement. They model the beliefs, values, and norms of behaviour which differentiate it from other movements. But why do they put such time and effort into this exemplary activity? Any explanation has to consider the nature of movements in general as social systems. Movements tend to concentrate on achieving a single or a very few aims, their basic purpose which defines them. This is in contrast to institutions, which have deeper historic roots and have developed a wider range of relationships with other institutions and social systems.

Fundamentalist movements, I have argued, have two basic aims: to obey God's Word, and to struggle against his enemies. These aims require beliefs, values, and norms to lead to actions designed to achieve them, both for the individual adherent and for the movement as a whole. The prototypical model acted out by leaders provides a clear template for adherents to follow. Further, since adherents tend to identify with leaders as personifications of the social identity of believer, they are likely to be motivated to conform to the prototype which he exemplifies (1). Such conformity has several benefits, both for individual adherents and for the movement itself.

First, *individual* adherents enjoy the satisfaction of several needs if they conform. The first is their need for meaning (2), since they are now completely confident that the beliefs, values, and norms to which they are committed are God's truth. Further, they meet their needs for affiliation, social approval, and self-esteem by their social identification and continuous association with other equally conformist adherents like themselves.

The outcomes of conformity for *movements* are varied. One is obvious: if adherents share the same beliefs, values, and norms, then they are more willing to take the same united action on the movement's behalf and as persuaded by its leaders. Another benefit relates to

DOI: 10.4324/9781003471981-16

differentiation (3). Differentiation from other movements is crucial to survival and success. However, if adherents do not conform to the prototype but rather vary according to their own preferences, then such differentiation will be less clear. There is no sharp distinction possible when the movement boundaries have fuzzy edges due to a variety of different beliefs. As a result, it becomes less easy to contrast the movement with its enemies and therefore to motivate adherents to struggle against a stereotypical Them.

There are, however, some downsides to conformity. If there is no dissenting minority, any change in the movement necessary if the fundamentalism is to survive is unlikely to occur (4). Even an innovative and adaptable leader may fail to institute change if he can find no existing supporters for it among the membership. Moreover, so much time and effort may go into enforcing conformity that other essential functions, for example, attracting new converts, may suffer as a result. Indeed, rigid conformity requirements may themselves put off potential converts. They may realise that once they commit, they are unlikely to take the huge step of reneging.

Pressures to conform

But leaders who model the movement's beliefs, values, and norms are not the only motivators of conformity. Other adherents also ensure that their colleagues toe the line. Like their leaders, believers too offer a model for others to follow, particularly for new converts who need to learn new beliefs, values, and norms but who may be at a loss as to what these are and what they imply in practice (5). Believers can also bring other adherents back into line by expressing their approval of conformity and disapproval of non-conformity. If an individual wants to belong, then the withdrawal of acceptance and welcome by fellow believers is a powerful sanction.

However, if this fails to induce conformity, a range of sanctions of ever-increasing severity is also available for dissuading deviants. The Brethren, for example (6), expect an elder in the potential deviant's congregation to have a quiet word of advice. If this is not successful, the elders together might require a more formal account to be given by the errant member. Expulsion from congregational fellowship is the ultimate sanction. The Amish, likewise (7), give advice before resorting to the harsher method of shunning the non-conformist. The Taliban on the other hand, beat or even execute those whom they discover breaking God's law.

The strict boundaries and high barriers which fundamentalisms erect between themselves and the outside world also help to induce and maintain conformity among their adherents. These are designed to prevent alien beliefs, values, and practices from infiltrating the consciousness of believers, although the growth of social media makes this aim ever more difficult to achieve. Moreover, adherents learn to treat the outside world as stereotypical enemies, agents of Satan. They are consequently unlikely to be attracted to their beliefs or practices; indeed, they often treasure the disdain and ridicule with which they are treated by the world, since being the victims of such persecution confirms them as true believers and servants of God. They often signal their difference by dressing in a highly distinctive way.

My analysis so far has been from a social scientific perspective on conformity and the functions it may serve. Once again, however, it is important to return to the believers' own perspective. Conformity is the logical consequence of the two core fundamentalist beliefs. The first of these requires obedience to the absolute and timeless truth that is the Word of God. This truth implies, according to each particular fundamentalism's teachings, a particular set of belief systems. There is thus no escape from conforming, since the truth is absolute and timeless, so there is no possibility of deviance or change. Conformity is often construed as imposed and enforced externally on the individual. However, in the case of the individual fundamentalist believer, it may be practised as a logical outcome of the first core belief. The same is true of the second. If one believes that one is in a constant struggle with the world, a battle between Us and Them, then clear differentiation of Us from Them is vital to success. Conformity to beliefs, values, and norms is necessary to ensure differentiation. It also motivates and justifies the conflict.

Conformity in action

But how is conformity established and maintained at the local level? What are the typical authority structures and processes which are in place in fundamentalist churches and mosques and synagogues, and associated organisations and groups? Two case studies of American Protestant fundamentalist congregations carried out by David Harrington Watt (8) and Joseph Tamney (9) illustrate their variety.

The first of these is the Philadelphia Church of Christ, part of the International Churches of Christ (Boston Movement). This movement was founded by its charismatic leader Kip McKean in 1979 and has kept considerable central control of its network of churches. Authority is vested in individuals at different levels within each congregation, with the pastor or minister at the pinnacle and deferred to in every situation. However, there is an extensive network of authority beneath him.

The distinguishing feature of the movement is the system of "discipling". Individual members are paired with an older and more experienced member. The parties are expected to meet face-to-face weekly and to be in contact daily. The junior partner is encouraged to tell their "discipler" about every aspect of their life and to abide by the directions which they were given. Membership of the Church is conditional on being in a disciple relationship. Mixed gender pairings are not permitted: women are supposed to submit to the authority of men, so could never be the senior partner; and anyway, they might tempt men to stray, so should not be in a disciple relationship with them at all. The health of the junior partner's marriage is of particular concern to their discipler, as the church is anxious to preserve, strengthen, and improve marriages. Husbands love your wives, and wives obey your husbands, is the key advice to be followed here. Disciplers are expected to pass on information gained from their meetings to church leaders if it is considered to be important.

Women, however, are not deprived of authority. Some of them are employed by the church as counsellors, who are responsible for the spiritual welfare of the other women in the church, and lead groups of women in Bible study and discussion. Others, however, devote themselves to helping their husbands in their church work, particularly if their husband is the pastor. And women are not allowed to perform the traditional offices of the church, nor even to speak in mixed gender meetings or worship services.

The second case study is of "Truth Church", a congregation in the city of Muncie, Indiana. This is better known as "Middletown", the name it was given in an early groundbreaking sociological study of a "typical white Anglo-Saxon culture". It is a classic example of a Calvinist fundamentalist congregation. As in the previous example, the minister has complete authority. He is treated as an inspired interpreter of God's Word the Bible, being attributed with the expert knowledge of theology which the congregation admitted it lacked. The form of theology expounded is that of the Presbyterian denomination to which the congregation belongs, and which it believes is God's revealed truth which they should apply to their lives.

The church is organised into demographically based groups, for example, youth, young mothers, and bible study groups for men and women separately. The youth program is structured by age bands and emphasises biblical teaching (as interpreted by the church) regarding such touchstone moral issues as abortion, sex outside heterosexual marriage, divorce, and drug and substance abuse. As with all other groups within the church, it is assumed that the relationships established between group members and with the group leader will reinforce conformity. Members will try to be like the others and gain their acceptance and approbation as a result.

There are four levels of conformity of belief and commitment to the church. The first level is that expected of the pastor, who is intimately bound to, and knowledgeable about, the Westminster Creed and the denomination's Book of Order. The second consists of all office holders within the church, who are expected to be committed but less knowledgeable. Church members, the third level, have to attend a membership class for about ten weeks and be interviewed by church elders before they are admitted. At this interview, they have to testify to their conversion experience and its consequences for their way of life. And the fourth level are attenders, who are free to attend any church activity, but cannot receive Holy Communion. This gradual progression within the church is likely to establish and then reinforce conformity with its beliefs, values, and norms. On the other hand, a degree of variety of interpretation of Biblical texts is permitted, but certainly not any questioning of the core beliefs or their immediate implications.

These two case studies illustrate the variety of ways in which fundamentalist Protestant congregations actively encourage conformity. Both of them are based on the reality that their adherents are also part of "the world", in the sense that they participate daily in many of the social systems of American society. However, there are other fundamentalisms which seek to enforce conformity through every single group or social system of which their adherents are a part. The Haredim and the Amish, for example, have separate housing, education, work, and social systems from everyone else. They do not even venture into the world to proselytise. What generalisations then, if any, can we make about how fundamentalisms organise so as to achieve their aims and objectives? The next chapter addresses this question.

Questions for discussion

1 Think of two social movements known to you, one of which is highly conformist and the other much less so. How successful is each in achieving its aims? Is success related to degree of conformity?
2 What sanctions have you observed in movements with which you are familiar? How effective were they, and why?
3 What hope do any non-conforming adherents have of exercising influence on fundamentalist movements? How might they succeed in doing so?

References

1. Turner, John (1991) Social Influence. Milton Keynes: Open University Press.
2. Hogg, Michael (2002) Social identity. In Leary, Mark & Tangney, June (eds.) Handbook of Self and Identity. New York: Guilford.
3. Brewer, Marilynn (2009) Motivations underlying ingroup identification: Optimal distinctiveness and beyond. In Otten, Sabine, Sassenberg, Kai & Kessler, Thomas (eds.) Intergroup Relations: The Role of Motivation and Emotion. Hove: Psychology Press.

4. Moscovici, Serge, & Mugny, Gabriel (1983) Minority influence. In Paulhus, Paul (ed.) Basic Group Processes. New York: Springer-Verlag.
5. Hogg, Michael & Mullin, Barbara-Ann (1999) Joining groups to reduce uncertainty: Subjective uncertainty reduction and group identification. In Abrams, Dominic & Hogg, Michael (eds.) Social Identity and Social Cognition. Oxford: Blackwell.
6. Herriot, Peter (2018) The Open Brethren: A Christian Sect in the Modern World. Cham, Switzerland: Palgrave Macmillan.
7. Hood, Ralph, Hill, Peter, & Williamson, Paul (2005) The Psychology of Religious Fundamentalism. New York: Guilford Press.
8. Watt, David (2002) Bible-Carrying Christians: Conservative Protestants and Social Power. New York: Oxford University Press.
9. Tamney, Joseph (2002) The Resilience of Conservative Religion: The Case of Popular Conservative Protestant Congregations. Cambridge: Cambridge University Press.

Further reading

Turner, John (1991) Social Influence. Milton Keynes: Open University Press.

Harding, Susan (2000) The Book of Jerry Falwell: Fundamentalist Language and Politics. Princeton: Princeton University Press.

Boston, Robert (2000) Close Encounters with the Religious Right: Journeys into the Twilight Zone of Religion and Politics. New York: Prometheus Books.

12 Organisation

Organisation and beliefs

Organisation is a modern preoccupation. It embodies values which are prioritised in the modern world. Modernity values instrumentality, that is, creating and marshalling the means to achieve a specific objective or purpose. It also values rationality: having good reasons for actions or policies, such as the evidence of previous outcomes and the probability of future ones given the circumstances. Hence, its preferred mode of operating is impersonal and rule-based, with any organisational role or function remaining the same whoever fills it. Or at least, that's the theory of bureaucratic organisation. Of course, this is not to say that organisation did not exist before the modern era. The history of the Chinese and the Roman Empires clearly argue otherwise. But as a pillar of every modern social system, it constitutes one of the foundations of modernity. Despite their continuous harking back to a pure and glorious golden age, fundamentalist movements are no exception. They too depend for their existence and success on organising well, and in this respect, as well as others, are essentially modern in nature.

How, then, do fundamentalist movements organise? In this chapter, I argue that the way they organise is, once again, a consequence of their two core beliefs. They have two central aims: to obey God's Word, and to struggle with his enemies. These aims determine the form of organisation which they adopt. However, movements interpret God's Word differently, with the result that the two core beliefs become translated into many different objectives, which in their turn require different forms of organisation. As a result, there is no single organisational form or structure which typifies fundamentalism. We may nevertheless distinguish certain general forms of organisation which reflect these objectives and the strategies devised to achieve them (1).

The most basic difference in strategy has permeated the previous chapters. It is that between *defensive and offensive*, separation and involvement, Brethren and Taliban. Depending on their context, movements with an offensive strategy may pursue it using *violent* means, such as terrorism, or *political* ones, such as "culture wars". Whatever their strategy, they all have to recruit adherents, acquire resources, and achieve objectives. But the ways in which they organise in order to pursue these strategic directions necessarily differ. What, then, are the organisational structures and processes favoured by defensive, politically offensive, and violently offensive fundamentalist movements, respectively?

Defensive organisation

Defensive fundamentalisms have separation and purity as their main aims, obeying God by avoiding sin. Their organisational structure is consequently designed to maintain strict obedience and conformity within the movement and erect strong barriers against the influence of the sinful world. It is not only the hierarchical authority structure which is imposed, however, but also a network of inter-related social systems which relate to every aspect of life. The movement may organise not only adherents' religious practices, but also their family life, education, neighbourhood location, occupations, and relations with the state.

The Amish, for example (2, 3), establish self-contained and largely self-reliant communities predominantly in rural locations in order to farm. They are so concerned that their members adhere to the movement's interpretation of the Bible that they discourage personal Bible study in favour of teaching by an elder. This teaching is strongly oriented towards social virtues such as humility, simplicity, and mutuality practised within the community. Regulations prohibiting the use of common elements of modern life are enforced (phones, cars, televisions etc), resulting in their popular stereotype as quaint throwbacks. However, these prohibitions are intended as symbolic assertions of their rejection of modern materialistic values.

Enforcement of obedience is achieved within each local Amish community by advice for a rule-breaker from a single fellow adherent, failing which a group will confront him or her. Continued unrepentance results in a public warning in front of the community, with the final step being excommunication and shunning. The latter results in the individual's family as well as other community members isolating them socially. The prime purpose is to signal the central importance of purity. The ordinances which these sanctions are designed to support are created by the movement's central leadership, not at individual community level.

Family structure and principles are closely tied to education. Amish are legally permitted in the United States to run their own schools, frequently with one schoolroom for the whole age range of children in the community. Both family life and education are concerned to cultivate the movement's favoured virtues. Parental authority is emphasised, and families are large as a result of the discouragement of birth control. As a consequence, they have no need to proselytise to maintain or increase their numbers, thereby avoiding the risk of contamination by those whom they might otherwise have tried to convert. And they manage to retain by far the greater proportion of their youth, partly by asking them to reaffirm their commitment after having given them permission to tentatively explore the outside world to see if they might prefer it.

Equally thoroughly organised internally are the Haredim (4). They too have a closely interlocking web of social systems, and once again family, education, location, and work combine together to ensure a movement that is insulated against its surrounding environment at every turn. They have succeeded in gaining support for their separation by securing special status with the Israeli government. Until recently they have been permitted to avoid military service, and the men have been supported in their sacred studies of the Torah throughout adulthood. After all, they believe that the redemption of Israel by the Messiah depends upon their understanding of and obedience to the Torah and all the legal regulations derived from it. They don't have the same opportunities as the Amish to live apart in a rural backwater, but they have succeeded in making specific neighbourhoods in cities into densely populated enclaves, even putting symbolic boundaries around them. Certainly, the Sabbath is better observed within them, and the Haredim's close obedience of the dress requirements also differentiates them clearly from other districts – a people apart.

Education is conducted within the enclave, with very few disciplines taught other than Torah study. Those secular skills which are acquired are usually exercised within businesses run entirely by Haredim. Many of these paid jobs are actually carried out by women, when they are not bearing children. Like the Amish, the Haredim have extremely high birth rates, with families of six or seven children being commonplace. A frequent estimate is that over 20 per cent of Jews in Israel will be Haredi by 2030. They have no need to proselytise, and they leave gentiles alone, whilst encouraging other less ultra-orthodox Jews to join them. However, their grip on their youth may be loosening under the pressure of the internet, and especially social media. Rabbis may seek to regulate the use of media, but efforts to order the lives of their children by the common practice of arranged marriages may become decreasingly successful.

The organisational similarities between the Amish and the Haredim are startling, with the key feature being the tight inter-connections between the different social systems so that family, education, work, and location all contribute to the defensive and separatist strategy. Their continuing growth may be attributed mainly to their high birth and retention rates. It is also worth noting that both have formal leadership operating above the level of their local communities, which is likely to

92 Social Foundations

result in a high level of conformity and hence of differentiation from other movements. Although defensive fundamentalisms seek to separate themselves and their youth from the world, the growth of social media enables unsupervised communication among the movement's youth and the accessing of uncensored material from outside. The high walls of the enclave may resist enemy bombardment, but they may find it much harder to keep out the deadly poison of the digital plague.

Politically offensive organisation

Many politically offensive fundamentalisms don't need to establish their own forms of organisation. This is because organisation already exists in the religious and political institutions of which they are part. They use this existing organisation in order to work against their own institution and if possible gain control of it. I have already referred repeatedly to American Protestant fundamentalists, who use the freedoms of democracy to struggle politically and non-violently to achieve objectives derived from their beliefs about moral issues. Instead, I will now describe a current struggle in the Australian Anglican Church, in order to point up fundamentalists' use of the internal structures and processes of their own institution to gain control (5, 6).

The Anglican Church in Australia has the same structure as the Church of England, with a Primate, archbishops, bishops, dioceses, and parishes, and is governed by a synod constituted of bishops, clergy, and laypersons. It also covers a broad range of theological positions, from Anglo-Catholicism to conservative Evangelicalism. The diocese of Sydney has long been a bulwark of Evangelicalism. However, from at least as far back as the 1990s, it has been the target of fundamentalists of an extreme Calvinist persuasion. Thus, the theological groundwork and the organisational structures and processes were already in place to facilitate a takeover bid. The fundamentalist strategy was patient and gradual, and its success by the early years of the new millennium was plain to see.

While the major feature of the takeover was gaining control of the structures of the church, the fundamentalists' more detailed organisational proposals are revealing. Their purpose was to point up the importance of certain of their theological beliefs, and to undermine the existing structures of denomination, diocese, parish, and priesthood accordingly. The first was their practice of *church planting* (unilaterally deciding from within a fundamentalist congregation to send out a group to establish a new church wherever there was an opportunity for evangelism). This threatened the existing parish and diocesan boundaries and often ignored the authority of the bishop. Moreover, there was no guarantee that the plant would follow Anglican rules and disciplines.

It expressed in action the belief dating back to the Reformation that congregations are the fundamental unit of the church, and that all other church systems are designed to support them.

A second organisational innovation was an apparently minor liturgical change – the extension of the ability to *administer Holy Communion* to deacons and lay people, rather than reserving it for ordained clergy. Again, this was aimed at the traditional view of the priesthood as responsible for the major rituals of the church. As far as the fundamentalists were concerned, these were of minor importance relative to the preaching of the Word of God. The refusal of the highest court of Australian Anglicanism to permit lay or diaconal presidency over Communion gave the by now fundamentalist diocese of Sydney the opportunity to defy the court's authority.

Another revealing organisational change was the takeover of Moore College, the dominant theological institution in Sydney. All teaching was now from the fundamentalist perspective. This signalled that there were no alternative perspectives on theology, but rather, one correct one. Graduating ordinands were expected to promulgate this party line when they were appointed "pastors" of congregations. This absolutist belief clearly carried implications for relationships with other Anglicans, other denominations, and other faiths.

The methods used to achieve these organisational changes, and more generally to gain control of the Anglican diocese of Sydney, were the time-honoured techniques of politics the world over. Pressure groups and caucuses were formed to exercise persuasion and win votes in the Sydney synod. Appointments to key leadership positions were achieved by an agreement on one candidate to represent the fundamentalist slate. Then, having been elected, they were to use their positional power to influence other appointments, for example, to be vicar of an important parish. It is interesting how many of the holders of these positions were surnamed Jensen!

Considerable fundamentalist effort was also put into pursuing conflict over the culture war topics of women priests and bishops and homosexuality, which bedevilled the Anglican Communion world-wide from the 1980s on. Archbishop Peter Jensen of Sydney spent considerable time and resources on supporting the mostly African bishops who fought these culture wars at successive Lambeth Conferences. He and his brother Philip, Dean of St Andrew's Cathedral, also allied Sydney with the Calvinist English pressure groups such as Reform and Anglican Mainstream. These seek to establish an alternative organisation to the Anglican Communion presided over by the Archbishop of Canterbury (7).

The Sydney story illustrates the advantages which the prior existence of institutional organisation gives to fundamentalist movements, like cuckoos taking over the nest. It also demonstrates the ways in which control of a religious institution can be the springboard for wider and more ambitious projects.

Violently offensive organisation

As soon as violence is associated with fundamentalism, Islamic terrorism comes to mind. However not all religious violence is terrorist; and not all terrorism is Islamist. No major world religion is any more prone to violence than the rest. If we define terrorism as violent attempts to terrify people into submission by means of indiscriminate murders, then much violent activity does not fall into this category. Rather, it consists of military attacks in an effort to conquer and annex territory and establish theocratic rule, as with ISIS in Iraq and the Taliban in Afghanistan. Furthermore, terrorist attacks have been carried out by militant Christians, Hindus, Jews, and sundry cults as well as by Islamists.

The proportion of fundamentalists who engage in terrorist violence is far smaller than is suggested by the media coverage and popular attention which they attract. It is also understandable that commentators have often sought to differentiate them sharply from the vast law-abiding majority of fundamentalist adherents. But however different al-Qaeda undoubtedly is from the Amish, I argue that they share together with all fundamentalists the same core belief which justifies and motivates their actions: that they are engaged in a cosmic struggle for their very survival. They draw utterly different conclusions about its implications for action, however.

A rather more nuanced account of terrorism than the brief definition above will demonstrate why its organisation is specific to its aims and objectives. Fundamentalists define cosmic war in a variety of ways. Some see it as a defensive spiritual war against the secular world; others as a political offensive designed to reform society; and others yet again as a military assault on the territory and forces of infidels. For terrorists, however, the war is above all *symbolic* (8). Its main objective is to assault the symbols of the enemy's power: the buildings which boast the importance of worldly institutions, or the daily business of the world's great cities full of depravity and sin. These assaults send the message that their perpetrators are capable of far worse and demonstrate the vulnerability of the supposedly invincible servants of Satan who had humiliated and persecuted the faithful. Far from avoiding attention, terrorists are delighted when they attract it, for the world's attention is necessary for their message to get across.

The images of terrorist acts are immediately broadcast globally. This boosts the morale of the faithful and acts as a recruitment tool for the young recruits who are willing to become foot-soldiers and martyrs in the cause. Recruitment can occur via social media, but the stereotype of the internet grooming and radicalisation of individuals is not strongly supported by research (9). Rather, existing kinship and friendship networks form the basis for many potential terrorist groups. Then, social media activity instils a picture of an imagined global community of believers (for Islamists, the umma). The idea of belonging to a global movement is affirmed when recruits are trained in the company of others from all over the world, all of whom believe themselves to have been persecuted and are hungry for revenge (10).

In order to conduct such challenging projects as 9/11, a structured and hierarchical form of organisation was initially required (11). The figurehead leader, anointed by the Almighty, developed a leadership cadre and project managers, who supervised skilled operatives and foot-soldiers eager for martyrdom. However, such a structured group is vulnerable to sophisticated counter-terror apparatus, as several terror groups such as al-Qaeda have more recently discovered. Terrorist organisations have become less formal and are characterised as networks of networks with minimal communications and a much more opportunistic mode of operation. The power of ideological belief is still real, however, despite being virtual. Indeed, the powerful and ubiquitous metaphor of war has ranged broadly in this chapter and has influenced organisation accordingly. From its mainstream religious usage referring to the spiritual struggle which each believer wages within their own life between obeying God or yielding to the temptations of Satan, it has morphed at the hands of terrorists into the self-righteous slaughter of anyone who is not a true believer, one of us.

Questions for discussion

1 Organisation is one feature of fundamentalism which is essentially modern. Which others occur to you, and why do you think they are important to its success?
2 Is there a long-term future for defensive fundamentalisms?
3 What strategies might mainstream religious institutions best employ to withstand the efforts of fundamentalisms to subvert and take control of them?
4 Do recent developments in information technology make fundamentalist terrorism more likely to succeed? How might it best be used to defeat it?

References

1. Almond, Gabriel, Appleby, Scott, & Sivan, Emmanuel (2003) Strong Religion: The Rise of Fundamentalism around the World. Chicago: University of Chicago Press.
2. Hostetler, John (1993) Amish Society (4th edn.) Baltimore: Johns Hopkins University Press.

3. Kraybill, Donald (2001) The Riddle of Amish Culture. Baltimore: Johns Hopkins University Press.
4. Janner-Klausner, Laura (2016) Jewish Fundamentalism. In Dunn, James (ed.) Fundamentalisms: Threats and Ideologies in the Modern World. London: IB Tauris.
5. McGillion, Chris (2005) The Chosen Ones: The Politics of Salvation in the Anglican Church. Crows Nest, New South Wales: Allen & Unwin.
6. Porter, Muriel (2011) Sydney Anglicans and the Threat to World Anglicanism. Farnham, Surrey: Ashgate.
7. Herriot, Peter (2016) Warfare and Waves: Calvinists and Charismatics in the Church of England. Eugene, OR: Wipf & Stock.
8. Juergensmeyer, Mark (2003) Terror in the Mind of God: The Global Rise of Religious Violence (3rd edn.) Berkeley: University of California Press.
9. Sageman, Marc (2004) Understanding Terror Networks. Philadelphia: University of Pennsylvania Press.
10. Gerges, Fawaz (2005) The Far Enemy: Why Jihad Went Global. New York: Cambridge University Press.
11. Stern, Jessica (2003) Terror in the Name of God: Why Religious Militants Kill. New York: Harper Collins.

Further reading

Juergensmeyer, Mark (2003) Terror in the Mind of God: The Global Rise of Religious Violence (3rd edn.). Berkeley: University of California Press.

Almond, Gabriel, Appleby, Scott, and Sivan, Emmanuel (2003) Strong Religion: The Rise of Fundamentalism around the World. Chicago: University of Chicago Press.

Part V
Perspectives
Past, Present, and Future

13 Modernity

Differentiation

The three most important questions about fundamentalism cannot be avoided any longer. Why did religious fundamentalist movements develop in the first place? Why do they continue to attract and retain considerable numbers of adherents? And what is their likely future? And I will suggest the following answers. Fundamentalisms were a reaction against modernity. They continue to flourish because modernity has not delivered on some of its prospectus. And they will certainly not fade away when the world's problems become ever more threatening. The final three chapters take these three temporal perspectives – past, present, and future. What follows in this final part of the book is a personal point of view. As a psychologist with a smattering of sociology and theology and minimal history, economics, and politics, I have no academic authority to address these issues. I merely present my own perspective in the hope that it will raise some key issues and stimulate discussion.

The study of modernity and its relationship with religion has generated a bewildering array of overlapping concepts (1). We have, first, the process of *modernisation* itself, divided temporally into segments of premodernity, modernity, late modernity, and post-modernity. Modernisation is generally considered a global process, a road along which different societies have travelled different distances. As a consequence, it is not usually represented as in binary tension with an opposite and countervailing process; it merely faces periodic reactionary opposition.

Other key and overlapping concepts, however, are all related to binary opposite terms. *Differentiation* refers to the original separating out of functional social systems such as government, law, science, religion, and business, and their further division into sub-systems or other systems. It has as its binary opposite integration. *Secularisation* (2) is used in different senses relating to religion (3). It is employed as a synonym for differentiation and also to refer to the consequent decline in religion's influence. It is contrasted with de-secularisation (4). And

DOI: 10.4324/9781003471981-19

finally *globalisation* is generally contrasted with localisation, treating functional social systems as global entities, and postulating a general global social system.

Faced with such numerous, inter-related, and vigorously contested theoretical concepts, my own preferred narrative has *differentiation* as its central idea. The modern world, in contrast with the pre-modern, is characterised by the process of constant differentiation. The basic differentiated function systems (5) such as business, government, science, law, and religion became consciously and purposefully distinct from each other over the course of the last three or four centuries. This self-awareness and self-development were very different from the pre-modern assumption that power was vested in the aristocracy and the church as the natural God-given order of things. They were prompted by such revolutionary cultural shifts as the Enlightenment, the Reformation, and the Industrial Revolution, and driven by such values as progress, equality, freedom, rationality, discovery, tolerance, and human rights.

Each function system had a central aim. For *business,* for example, this was the creation of wealth, for *government,* the acquisition and use of power, for *science*, the discovery of new truth, for *law,* the pursuit of justice, and for *religion*, an appreciation of the transcendent. Each function system's aim determined the nature of its main activity: buying and selling, regulating and decision-making, collecting data and theorising, interpreting and enforcing laws, and piety and ritual, respectively. Given this single-minded pursuit of its particular aim and given its concentration on the appropriate instrumental activity, it is not surprising that each system developed its own unique culture. It developed, in other words, its own relatively coherent set of beliefs, values, and practices. Function systems were primarily concerned to reproduce themselves and ensure their continuity. So concerned were they with their internal culture that they developed a language and symbols which were often impenetrable to outsiders.

One of the most important features of these different cultures is the variety of criteria which they used to assess whether something is true or not. Science, for example, employs very different truth criteria from the religious or legal systems. Science requires reproducible empirical evidence, religion cites revelation, authority, and experience, while the law asks for evidence beyond reasonable doubt. This variety is difficult to accept, because it denies our preferred binary clarities: either something is true or else it's false, we want to believe.

If this level of differentiation is the basic characteristic of modernity, how has modern humankind adapted to it? How is the global differentiated social system represented in the mind of its citizens? A standard response, as proposed in chapter 7, is to suggest that each individual embraces certain social identities, that is, beliefs that they belong to specific social categories: religious believer, law-abiding citizen, scientist, and American, for example. But the beliefs, values, and practices of these social systems may well be incompatible, or at least very different. Science needs empirical observation, for example, religion requires revelation, the law establishes precedents, and nationalism depends on loyalty. So how does the modern person maintain any degree of personal integrity? If they merely play the appropriate social role in any situation, without actually buying into the culture, they may feel and appear inauthentic (6). Perhaps, it is suggested, a strong *personal and individual identity* can over-ride the contradictions among disparate social identities. In any event, modern people have somehow adapted themselves to the rapid differentiation of the functional systems.

As function systems generate ever greater wealth, knowledge, power, and piety, they differentiate out into more and more sub-systems. It seems obvious that new areas of expertise will emerge, each with their own membership, and sometimes even entire new function systems will form. Arguably, social media is one such recent addition. Overall, this account of modernity as differentiation hangs together well: in fact, far too well. It is much too neat and tidy and rational, a truly modern account of modernity. The reality may be much more messy.

Integration

But what of the other side of the differentiation coin? Continuous differentiation results in additional boundaries within and between systems, resulting in decreased communication and collaboration. Within systems, boundaries form both sideways with other sub-systems and upward to the parent system. For example, new academic specialisms are desperate to differentiate themselves from related specialisms and often eager to break free from the rules and restrictions set by their parent discipline. A moment's reflection, however, indicates that such fantasies of independence are indeed delusions. The adventurous psychologist, for example, soon realises that their "new" specialism is the outcome of theories and methods already developed by their parent discipline. *Successful differentiation is only possible if it is balanced by appropriate integration.* Integration reflects the fact that different systems and sub-systems actually depend on each other if they are to successfully achieve their own aim. The law, for example, depends on government for protection from threat and for resources, but in return it provides legitimacy for government and a law-abiding context for other systems such as business to function successfully. At the same time, however, it has to hold government and business to account. Similarly, business and government depend on science and technology to develop their products and services, but science needs their financial support in order to function at all. This very dependence, however, threatens its objectivity.

How, then, does *religion* fit into this differentiation/integration narrative? It has certainly achieved separate and differentiated status as a function system. However, this "achievement" has been largely forced upon it by other systems as they sought to emphasise their independence from the control of the pre-modern religious elite. Several nation states have explicitly excluded religion from the public sphere in their constitutions, for example, France. And the medical system is extremely hostile to the threat to its authority posed by so-called faith healing. However, this hostility has not stopped religion from seeking to exercise influence in the public sphere, for example, in matters of social morality and justice. The Archbishop of Canterbury has recently used his membership of the British Parliament's House of Lords as Head of the established Anglican Church to seek to moderate the provisions of harsh immigration legislation.

Like other function systems, religion is concerned to differentiate itself from other systems and to reproduce itself. It is particularly subject to internal differentiation, as sects divide and subdivide freely. It has, however, also succeeded in integrating itself to the extent that it is recognised by other systems as a global system, incorporating global institutions such as the World Council of Churches. But in terms of its relationship with other systems, integration is more problematic. Sometimes religion has gained resources and power from government by supporting its policies regardless of their direction. Current examples are the support of the Russian Orthodox Church for Putin's invasion of Ukraine, and of American Evangelicalism for Trump. In these cases, religion provides legitimacy and voters for the powerful. In general, however, the major function systems do not feel they need anything which religion can provide. They have not been averse, on the other hand, to subjecting religion to analysis and control. Indeed, fundamentalism originated with American Protestants' reaction against the academic use of techniques of textual analysis on the Bible (7).

However, religion's relative lack of integration with other increasingly powerful systems does not appear to have resulted in its inevitable and universal decline, as predicted by the *secularisation* thesis. On the contrary, while it has declined in Europe, it is expanding in the global South (8). Furthermore, as I will argue in the next chapter, conservative religion is playing a dominant role in the current global growth of authoritarian populist nationalist regimes. However, the generally accepted account of the origin of fundamentalism as a reaction against modernity is a convincing one. Religion has lost its pre-modern functions and power, often with a great unwillingness. Moreover, many religious institutions object to the core values of modernity as established in the Enlightenment and as expressed in the narrative of modernity as progress in the ability to solve problems and improve the human condition. There is, however, an *alternative narrative of modernity* which portrays it as currently failing to fulfil much of its prospectus, with a consequent loss of certainty and security, agency, and self-esteem. *In this latter account, fundamentalism today is not so much a reaction against modernity's historical successes as against its recent failures.*

Modernity's failures

It seems perverse to accuse modern function systems of failing when health, wealth, opportunity, and mobility have vastly increased globally during their continued development (9). However, there are several crucial ways in which they are undermining the common good. The first concerns their *over-emphasis on themselves*. Each function system is at constant risk of treating its own maintenance and promotion as its primary concern, concentrating on its own differentiation rather than on integration with other systems and with the global social system itself. Systems are extremely self-referential, or, to borrow a term from the study of fundamentalism, intra-textual. So, for example, they measure their success in terms of their own activities. They calculate number of papers published in scientific journals, or number of converts added to the faith, or size of dividends paid to shareholders. There is much less reference to successful collaborations with other systems aimed at increasing the common good.

A second shortcoming of the upbeat narrative of modernity and progress is its failure to recognise and address *the issue of power* (10). There are massive power differentials both within and between function systems. A very few nations are global giants, and their governments are sometimes autocratic and unaccountable. Powerful global corporations, especially high tech and fossil fuel companies, are threatening the fabric of society and indeed the very existence of humankind. The media are dominated by a very few major players, who manipulate public opinion to reflect the opinions of their owners. These and other inequalities of power have pernicious consequences, since they result in further forms of inequality. There are massive and increasing differences in wealth, health, and general well-being. For example, the majority of wealthy people became rapidly wealthier during the recent pandemic, while the remainder stood still or became poorer. Such growing inequalities naturally result in increased feelings of alienation from society, as modernity's promise of general progress is tarnished. Cynicism regarding societal institutions is common, and conspiracy theories flourish.

When function systems do integrate with others, the reason is generally in order to *promote their own continued existence*. Science collaborates with business, for example, science surviving on the investment and resourcing supplied by business, and business on the profits derived from technology. Religion needs the security provided by government if it is to survive and flourish, and governments sometimes depend for their survival on the support and legitimacy conferred by religion. However, a far greater threat to the global social system occurs when function systems collaborate in order to acquire excessive combined power. For example, totalitarian governments regularly ally with high-tech corporations in order to spy upon and deceive their own citizens.

Another disturbing feature of modernity is the *increasing pace* of growth and development of the function systems. In their bid to achieve their basic aims of generating more wealth, power, or knowledge, they are racing ahead within their respective silos with minimal input from other systems or civil society. Particular examples are the current unregulated development of artificial intelligence, and the creation and marketing of untried financial instruments. The latter has already caused global recession, whereas the former has only just begun to demonstrate its outcomes. But in both these cases and in others, people have difficulty in understanding the nature and implications of such rapid change and feel that anyway they have no influence on its nature or direction. In psychological terms, they lose meaning, agency, and self-esteem, thereby making themselves possible recruits for fundamentalist movements.

There are then, in summary, two possible ways in which the differentiation and related integration of functional systems, the essence of modernity, might be implicated in the growth of fundamentalism. The first is people's realisation that other functional systems have, during the course of modernisation, taken away from religion much of the power, influence, and respect which it possessed in pre-modern times. And the second is their widespread perception that function systems are generally highly effective at achieving their major aims but are poor at ensuring that this success benefits the entire global social system and themselves as its members.

Questions for discussion

1 Choose a function system with which you are familiar. What is its major aim, and how does it seek to achieve it?
2 What are the major difficulties it faces, and which of these does it find most problematic? Why?
3 Now answer questions 1 and 2 in the case of religion.
4 What are the features of modernisation most likely to prompt the rise of fundamentalism? Why?

References

1. Beyer, Peter (2006) Religions in Global Society. London: Routledge.
2. Martin, David (2005) On Secularisation: Towards a Revised General Theory. Aldershot: Ashgate.
3. Casanova, Jose (1994) Public Religions in the Modern World. Chicago: University of Chicago Press.
4. Berger, Peter (1999) The Desecularisation of the World: A Global Overview. In Berger, Peter (ed.) The Desecularisation of the World: Resurgent Religion and World Politics. Grand Rapids, MI: William Eerdmans.
5. Juergensmeyer, Mark (2006) Religious Antiglobalism. In Juergensmeyer, Mark (ed.) Religion in Global Civil Society. New York: Oxford University Press.
6. Bauman, Zygmunt (1996) From Pilgrim to Tourist – Or a Short History of Identity. In Hall, Stuart & du Gay, Paul (eds.) Questions of Cultural Identity. London: Sage.
7. Carpenter, Joel (1997) Revive Us Again: The Reawakening of American Fundamentalism. New York: Oxford University Press.
8. Davie, Grace (2002) Europe: The Exceptional Case: Parameters of Faith in the Modern World. London: Darton, Longman, & Todd.
9. Pinker, Steven (2019) Enlightenment Now: The Case for Reason, Science, Humanism, and Progress. London: Penguin.
10. Runciman, David (2018) How Democracy Ends. London: Profile.

Further reading

Beyer, Peter (2006) Religions in Global Society. London: Routledge.
Smith, Graeme (2008) A Short History of Secularism. London: IB Tauris.
Norris, Pippa & Inglehart, Ronald (2004) Sacred and Secular: Religion and Politics Worldwide. Cambridge: Cambridge University Press.
Seligman, Adam (2000) Modernity's Wager: Authority, the Self, and Transcendence. Princeton: Princeton University Press.

14 Populism

National identity

In her dystopian futuristic masterpiece *The Handmaid's Tale* (1), Margaret Attwood predicted in 1985 the state of the world in which many live some 40 years later. She described a totalitarian society in which autocratic populist leadership was in alliance with religion. How has this come about? The failure of modernity to fully deliver on its prospectus was proposed in the previous chapter as a major cause of the current loss of meaning, security, agency, and self-esteem. This in turn has provided fertile psychological ground for fundamentalist movements. However, fundamentalism has not proved attractive to a high proportion of the world's population, despite its undoubted impact. The last two decades have instead seen the global growth of populist nationalism (2), another potent reaction against modernity.

Nationalism is not an attribute of the institution of the nation state, one of the pillars of modernity. Rather, it refers to a less defined and more intangible social identity – the belief that one belongs to a particular people. This identity often evokes feelings of nostalgia for a past national golden age and sometimes carries racial connotations. Nationalism can be *populist* (3, 4) in the sense that it equates the nation with the people. These are, according to nationalists, the "real" people, in contrast with the elites who run the modern institutions, the "woke" liberal intellectuals, and the shadowy cabal of (Jewish) financiers who control the world's economy. According to Viktor Orban of Hungary, such elites perceive those concepts to be irrational which have shaped and determined Europe and the lives of Europeans for two thousand years: concepts such as faith, nation, community, and family.

Populist leaders rely on the support of "the people", which they acquire and maintain by constantly attacking the institutions which underpin the vital function systems of society. They denigrate and seek to control the judiciary, the media, academia, and civil society, for example. And they scapegoat minority groups such as immigrants, the unemployed, and LGBT people, blaming them for the various misfortunes of "the real people". In no particular order, we may cite Trump, Orban, Erdogan, Modi, Bolsonaro, Meloni, and Netanyahu as examples of recent or current political leaders whom we could label populist in terms of these criteria. We can also identify prominent and powerful politicians in opposition to current governments who are eager to establish populist alternatives, for example, Marine Le Pen in France, Geert Wilders in the Netherlands, and Santiago Abascal in Spain.

However, the new factor is not so much populist nationalism as such, which has already caused the world untold historic suffering. It is rather its relationship with religion. It is immediately evident that the psychological foundations of populist nationalism are identical with those of religious fundamentalism as I have described it in previous chapters. Both nationalism and fundamentalism address the psychological problem of the loss of meaning and security, agency, and self-esteem, which is in large part the result of the failure of late modernity to meet the expectations of an increasing proportion of the world's population. They do so by exploiting the same psychological processes (5), as follows.

They first establish a social identity which constitutes a central element in the self-concept of their followers: the real people and God's people, respectively. They propagate prototypical models of the patriot and the believer, attributing such virtues as honesty, loyalty, and duty to the former, and purity, obedience, and conformity to the latter. In order to further differentiate their movements from others, they create *stereotypes* (6) of members of other movements and social systems, attributing to them the vices which are the opposite of their own virtues. The elite enemies of the nation, for example, are dishonest conspiratorial schemers and liberal ideologues, who care nothing for the faith and family virtues which hold it together. For fundamentalists, the evil world and its puppet master Satan are lustful degenerates who deliberately disobey God and each go their own sinful way. Thus, both nationalism and fundamentalism create an Us versus Them conflict based on a central highly rewarding identity which has to be defended against its enemies to the end.

Both populism and fundamentalism are therefore likely to attract people in search of a certain sort of story. They want a narrative which gives unambiguous answers to their uncertainties about the nature of the world they experience and their own position within it. They like to feel that they can do something about it by struggling against their supposed enemies. And they long to be somebody again in a world that they feel treats them as nobodies. They need, in other words, meaning, agency, and self-esteem, and both populism and fundamentalism seem to offer them.

Furthermore, both movements' narratives are *restorationist*. They look backwards nostalgically to a glorious golden age of national or spiritual splendour and imply that its restoration is within reach ("Make America Great Again"; "A Christian Europe"). This emphasis reflects the experience of many of their followers, who feel deeply the loss of social status or financial security which they previously enjoyed in better times and believe that authoritarian leadership will bring back. The role of *leadership* in the whole process is crucial psychologically (7). Followers can see their social identity as patriots or believers personified in their leader (despite many leaders coming from privileged backgrounds), bringing them hope and direction. Hope is desperately needed in order to enable them to come to terms with another dominant theme of the narrative: *victimhood and persecution*. The experience of persecution and the status of victim are a lynchpin of the narrative because it enables followers to confirm their enemies as those arrogant elites who conspire against them and put them down.

But the fact that populism and fundamentalism use the same basic psychological processes to attract, retain, direct, and motivate their similarly dispossessed followers is not a sufficient reason for suggesting that they are currently in league with each other. Rather, we have to examine the development and nature of the *relationship between populism and religion in general* at the present historical moment. It is unsurprising that different historical, political, and cultural contexts across the world make it impossible to come up with any universal explanation and lead rather to an appreciation of the varied forms of relationship involved.

Religious populism

However, I will risk gross oversimplification by suggesting that there are two main categories of this relationship. One form might be termed *"religious populism"*, in the sense that the senior and more powerful partner is populism. It is to be found in societies in which nationhood is now understood as an overarching concept incorporating religion as one of its core features. The narrative of nationhood assumes a national identity which is unchanging over time, being embedded in a historical culture and passed down by tradition. The importance for this identity of family, faith, and place is emphasised, with some historical justification in the case of faith. In the past, the institutions of religion have frequently cooperated politically with government and enjoyed the status of the established religion of the state.

This established status, however, has long ago become a shadow of its former self in the West, where any such relationship is now largely nominal (8); witness the Lutheran church in Germany and the Church of England. Why, then, the emphasis is on religion in populist nationalism? Once we recognise populist nationalism as a reactionary response to globalisation, with its threatening transnational institutions and its national multiculturalism, the answer becomes clear (9, 10). Nationalists fear for the survival of the very idea of nationhood and their own national narrative in particular. They react by seeking to re-establish it in its mythical form, of which religion is a fundamental pillar.

Despite all this air of golden age restorationism, however, populist nationalism in fact represents a powerfully new and radical assault on modernity and its institutions. It uses the religious institutions of its locale to add to its appeal to its core constituency. So, for example, Putin uses the Russian Orthodox Church to legitimise his invasion of Ukraine. Erdogan cultivates conservative Islam to maintain his power over secular opposition to his rule. Trump granted audience and status to Evangelical luminaries in order to ensure the electoral support of their congregations.

It is not possible, then, to characterise my first category of populism-religion relationships as consisting of an alliance between populism and fundamentalism. Populist movements and their leaders typically use long-established religious institutions such as the Roman Catholic or Orthodox Churches as dependent allies; however, one of the core features of fundamentalism is its hostility to mainstream religion, which it habitually treats as a heretical enemy. Moreover, the basic belief of fundamentalists is that God is the sole authority whose word must be obeyed. Few populist leaders claim that they are following God's will. No, they affirm noisily; it is the will of the people that they seek to carry out in order to defend the nation. So overall, the conclusion is that when it comes to my category of "religious populism", fundamentalism is not at present heavily involved.

Theocracy

The second category of current relations between the state and religion is usually termed *theocracy* and is based on a different set of historical and cultural conditions. Instead of the state using religion for its purposes, theocracy is the product of a fundamentalist takeover of political and other institutions. It has its origins in the colonial era, when imperial Western powers imposed their brand of modernity on their empires. The dominant element of this project was the establishment of secular nation states based on liberal Western models in such countries as Egypt, India, and Iran. This reproduction of Western political systems was imposed on these and other countries with little consideration of their particular social, cultural, and political histories. Specifically, it largely ignored the importance of historic tribal, clan, and religious social systems and loyalties (11).

The immediate benefits of secular nationhood were derived mainly from the impact of the imperial powers. They developed functional social systems in the modern mode, especially those of law, education, science and technology, and trade. However, this development was not perceived as motivated by a desire to compensate for imperial exploitation, but rather as a means of maintaining and extending Western power by political influence and alliances. Moreover, it became evermore evident over time that many of the rulers of the new secular states were governing corruptly and enriching themselves and their supporters at the expense of the general populace.

The impetus for resistance came from radical ideological Islamists such as Qutb (11) and Mawdudi. These clerics were able in typical fundamentalist fashion to brand nominally Muslim secular nation states as apostates and their Western supporters as infidels. This fundamentalist narrative was the ideological tinder which fuelled the development of a wide variety of radical organisations, such as the Muslim Brotherhood in Egypt, the Taliban in Afghanistan, Isis in Syria, and al-Qaeda. Where radical Islamists have gained power, as in Iran and Afghanistan, it was the clergy who claimed authority and dominated the institutions of government, law, commerce, and social conduct (see chapter 3). Thus, theocracies could justifiably be termed fundamentalist states.

In summary, the potential role of fundamentalist religion in the current development of populist nationalism is unclear. While absolutist belief in God's Word and the cosmic struggle which it ordains is the basic building block of fundamentalism, the central emphases of nationalism are local and nativist, and its authority is vested in its leaders, standing proxy for "the people". These are big differences to overcome. However, the identical nature of the psychological foundations of fundamentalism and nationalism and the similarity of their respective supportive constituencies make them potentially an immensely powerful bloc were they ever to ally. This eventuality nevertheless seems improbable. Fundamentalists continue to be motivated and directed by their core beliefs: their God has revealed himself to them by his Word; and it is their task to obey only him and struggle on his behalf against all others. He cannot be treated as simply part of the furniture of the national culture.

Questions for discussion

1 Is populist nationalism the greatest current social threat, or merely a favourite target of the liberal democratic West?
2 What difficulties are populist nationalists and fundamentalist believers likely to encounter if they try to collaborate, and why?
3 Why has fundamentalist belief been successful in turning certain secular nations into theocracies?

Populism 111

References

1. Attwood, Margaret (1985) The Handmaid's Tale. Toronto: McClelland & Stewart.
2. Grayling, Anthony (2017) Democracy and Its Crisis. London: Oneworld Publications.
3. Mudde, Cas & Kaltwasser, Cristobal (2017) Populism: A Very Short Introduction. New York: Oxford University Press.
4. Muller, Jan Werner (2016) What is Populism? Philadelphia, PA: University of Pennsylvania Press.
5. Herriot, Peter (2020) Populism, Fundamentalism, and Identity: Fighting Talk. Cham, Switzerland: Palgrave Macmillan.
6. Hogg, Michael & Abrams, Dominic (2003) Intergroup behaviour and social identity. In Hogg, Michael, & Cooper, Joel Handbook of Social Psychology. London: Sage.
7. Haslam, Alexander, Reicher, Stephen, & Platow, Michael (2011) The New Psychology of Leadership, Identity, Influence, and Power. Hove: Psychology Press.
8. Davie, Grace (2002) Europe: The Exceptional Case: Parameters of Faith in the Modern World. London: Darton Longman & Todd.
9. Juergensmeyer, Mark (2006) Religious antiglobalism. In Juergensmeyer, Mark (ed.) Religion in Modern Global Society. New York: Oxford University Press.
10. Gills, Barry (ed.) (2000) Globalization and the Politics of Resistance. Houndmills: Macmillan.
11. Qutb, Sayyid (2001) Milestones. New Delhi: Islamic Book Service.

Further reading

Mudde, Cas & Kaltwasser, Cristobal (2017) Populism: A Very Short Introduction. New York: Oxford University Press.
Runciman, David (2018) How Democracy Ends. London: Profile Books.
Davies, William (2020) This Is Not Normal: The Collapse of Liberal Britain. London: Verso.

15 Apocalypse

Popular apocalypse

Why, many readers may be asking, was the previous chapter concerned about populist nationalism? Surely there are much more important issues about which we should be immediately concerned – for example, the threatening approach of such horsemen of the apocalypse as climate disaster, pandemics, nuclear catastrophe, or artificial intelligence. But populist nationalism is with us already, and its results have been experienced widely. It is frequently interpreted as a current trend in national and global politics which arouses strong support and equally strong criticism. The horsemen of the apocalypse, however, are understood, appropriately enough, in an apocalyptic way. Their thundering hooves already sound in our ears and terrify us.

The *apocalyptic tradition* is derived from a variety of ancient religious beliefs (1). However, its modern popular usage can perhaps best be summarised by the common phrase "the end of the world as we know it". This usage is often accompanied by the phrase "existential threat". The general assumption is that the present state of affairs is so dire that apocalypse is the only possible future outcome. In other words, apocalypse is a way of making sense of present painful experience by projecting it into inescapable future catastrophe.

Whether or not apocalyptic beliefs are justified by current evidence is not an issue for discussion here. Other far more qualified commentators have emphasised the grounds for believing that the dangers are only too real. What is important for my argument is that they are widely held beliefs, and, to repeat *ad nauseam*, beliefs are the basis for behaviour. Moreover, they are now no longer arcane aspects of religious belief systems but constitute a basic world-view shared by large numbers of religious and secular people alike (2). The core belief of this world-view is that apocalypse is already determined; there is no escaping it. There are, however, major differences between religious and secular people regarding its causes and consequences.

In general, *religions* treat apocalypse as the inevitable outcome of God's plan for humankind. He has decided that Satan has had enough success deceiving people and seducing them into sin. He sends many signs and signals of the day of judgement to come, but they are ignored (3), so he comes in power and majesty. He destroys the powers of darkness and evil and establishes his kingdom of justice and peace on earth. While apocalypse involves terrible struggle and suffering, God's saved and redeemed people ultimately enjoy a perfect existence. Thus, religious people tend to attribute apocalypse and its consequences to God, although many add an element of human agency in the belief that they can hasten God's plan by their faithful efforts on his behalf. The religious account of apocalypse, then, offers the possibility of redemption and salvation, the hope of "a new heaven and a new earth".

Many *secular* people, however, attribute apocalypse to forces which they believe to be out of control and inevitable – science, progress, human nature, or fate, for example, or even religion. These attributions lead them to give up any hope of agency. Others may attribute the possibility of apocalypse to the faulty operation of function systems, for example blaming governments for colluding with tech corporations and fossil fuel companies, an attribution which in principle permits the avoidance of apocalypse by means of the reform of institutions. But apocalyptic belief generally denies the possibility of human action averting catastrophe and so results in helplessness and despair. It may even lead people to anticipate and act out what they perceive to be inevitable anyway. If disaster is assured, do whatever you've always really wanted to before it's too late, even if it brings doomsday closer. Alternatively, buy a bunker in the desert somewhere (4).

Fundamentalist apocalypse

The world's religions, then, probably have a less pessimistic apocalyptic narrative than secular perspectives. Religious narratives admit the terrible struggle and suffering of the end times but conclude with the hope of an ultimate golden age of justice and peace. *But what of fundamentalists?* How does their account of apocalypse differ from that of mainstream religion?

As with every other element of their lives, fundamentalists' apocalyptic narrative derives from their two core beliefs: in the Word of God and the necessity of struggle. They believe that God has spoken directly to them. All fundamentalists believe that God speaks clearly and that the sense which they have made of his Word is its only possible meaning. All who make a different interpretation are apostate believers, the most dangerous enemy of all. Hence, these "apostates", those of other religions and those of no religion at all, are all God's enemies, against whom he has commanded them to struggle. This struggle may sometimes involve building metaphorical walls to keep them out and maintain purity; but it is more likely to require political or violent action.

Hence, a fundamentalist narrative is likely to attribute apocalypse to omnipotent God, but to claim that only adherents of their own fundamentalism are his soldiers. They are his agents in visiting stern justice upon humankind. Not only are they his army who will destroy or control everyone on earth except themselves, however. They will also act as his regents in his kingdom of righteousness, administering his just punishment upon all his enemies. Thus, fundamentalists derive their narrative from mainstream religious apocalyptic beliefs. However, because of their absolutism and their hostility to all others, the hope of ultimate justice and peace which characterises the mainstream religious narrative is distorted into perversions of these desirable outcomes. Utopia becomes transformed into *a violent dystopia* (5). The struggles against Satan result not in an ultimate heaven on earth, but in a dreadful hell where fundamentalist believers rejoice in visiting their God's vengeance on everyone else, thereby purging their own feelings of humiliation. Of course, the looming horsemen of the apocalypse such as climate disaster, nuclear annihilation, pandemics, and artificial intelligence may bring violence with them. However, violence is not an intrinsic element of the fatalistic secular apocalyptic, as it is in most fundamentalist narratives.

The possibility therefore arises that many who are convinced by the secular account may consider that their only hope of avoiding extinction is to give up on the institutions of modernity which they believe to have failed them. Instead, they may turn to an alternative narrative, according to which only a great leader, who is willing and able to do whatever it takes to defeat their powerful enemies, can save the world from destruction. One such narrative is the fundamentalist story, which has the added advantage of replacing people's threatened social and personal identities with a dominant glorious identity as true believers, God's army (6). From this perspective, current secular fears of the end of the world provide a potentially fruitful context for a resurgence of violent fundamentalist adherence and belief.

How might this outcome be avoided? There are many possible actors who might take steps to prevent such an eventuality. I will concentrate only on what religion as a function system might contribute, given that, first, this is a book about religion; and second, religion is the original source of most apocalyptic narrative.

A new religious narrative

It is to the development and propagation of *narrative* that religion might well direct its efforts. A convincing narrative story can change minds and world-views, in contrast to the "on the one hand but on the other"

Apocalypse 115

discourse of us academics (7). Successful narratives deal in dramatic binaries, the classic example, of course, being "goodies versus baddies". Their success is partly due to the possibility of defining one of the binary terms by its opposite. If they are to create a narrative suited to countering the current fundamentalist one, the world's religions will have to make clear choices between several key binary terms and their opposites.

So which *binary terms* should religion support at the expense of their opposites? By what criteria should these be selected? One criterion surely has to be religion's own historical success in promoting terms which meet human needs, and which are needed even more today. Another might be that fundamentalists have misrepresented religion by choosing deeply damaging alternatives over their preferable opposites, causing false impressions which need correction. And finally, several functional social systems have chosen binary terms from which they derive dangerous narratives.

What, then, might be the key terms of a new religious narrative? Mainstream religions will rightly retain their traditional support of hope over despair, equity over inequality, love over hate, respect over contempt, forgiveness over revenge, and truth over falsehood, among others. But at the present historical moment, they would do well to disown fundamentalist distortions by emphasising inclusion over exclusion, enquiry over certainty, and dialogue over conflict. And they will counter various harmful narratives propagated by different function systems such as science and technology, business, and politics. This means, for example, choosing humility over arrogance, the latter exemplified by the scientific belief that humankind can understand and control the natural world and solve any problems which it faces (8). It also requires a preference for need over profit, the common good over personal interest (9), and service over power, addressing thereby some of the current faults of business and politics respectively.

The development of such a religious narrative is not simply a creative literary endeavour. *It is a theological, moral, social, and political act*. As such, it threatens the vested interests and power structures attached to other functional systems, although it also resonates with some of their beliefs and values. Through inviting existing and potential adherents to embrace an overall social identity as human beings and children of God, it may subsume other identities such as citizen and carer which are already internalised and valued. But it may also challenge other identities, such as consumer and winner, which are central elements of important economic and political narratives. If it makes these binary choices, religion may be attacked by other threatened function systems in retaliation for straying from its fundamental purpose. Governments, for example, may threaten it with state control or withdrawal of freedoms.

However, the purpose of a new religious narrative would not be to attack other social systems, but rather, *to gain greater general public acceptance*. Success with the public would therefore necessarily result in the decline in popularity of some of the narratives of other function systems which are incompatible with the new narrative. But public acceptance is not easy to come by. While personable internet "influencers" may successfully propagate their narratives at lightning speed, most institutions are now suspected as remote and distant and concerned only with power and position. In particular, they are perceived to defend themselves and their leaders at all costs and to be motivated by greed and ambition. Religious institutions are particularly susceptible to such charges, partly because their actions are judged by the criteria of their very demanding prospectus.

The high level of public cynicism regarding modern institutions is currently encouraged by populist politicians (10). But religion, like other function systems, has indeed sometimes recently been found to be failing to walk its talk and live by its prospectus. A powerful new narrative is therefore only part of the radical reform required. Without action, it is just mere words, to be distrusted or ignored, like all the other words and images which constantly demand our attention. But if it is consistent with practice, a new religious narrative is an essential contribution to an inspiring vision, not of apocalypse, but of justice and peace.

Questions for discussion

1 How and why do reasonable fears about the future become apocalyptic?
2 What are the most likely reasons why people might turn to fundamentalism in the present historical context? What are the probable consequences of such an increase in its popularity?
3 What are the main obstacles to religion creating a successful narrative account of the future?

References

1. Hall, John (2009) Apocalypse: From Antiquity to the Empire of Modernity. Cambridge: Polity Press.
2. Wojcik, Daniel (1997) The End of the World As We Know It: Faith, Fatalism, and Apocalypse in America. New York: New York University Press.
3. Boyer, Paul (1994) When Time Shall Be No More: Prophecy Belief in Modern American Culture. Cambridge, MA: Harvard University Press.
4. O'Connell, Mark (2020) Notes From An Apocalypse: A Personal Journey to the End of the World and Back. London: Granta.
5. Strozier, Charles, Terman, David, & Jones, James (2010) The Fundamentalist Mindset: Psychological Perspectives on Religion, Violence, and History. New York: Oxford University Press.

6. Herriot, Peter (2007) Religious Fundamentalism and Social Identity. Hove: Routledge.
7. Gubrium, Jaber & Holstein, James (2009) Analyzing Narrative Reality. Thousand Oaks, CA: Sage.
8. Harari, Yuval (2016) Homo Deus: A Brief History of Tomorrow. London: Vintage Books.
9. Roemer, John (1996) Theories of Distributive Justice. Cambridge, MA: Harvard University Press.
10. Moffitt, Benjamin (2016) The Global Rise of Populism: Performance, Political Style, and Representation. Stanford, CA: Stanford University Press.

Further reading

Wojcik, Daniel (1997) The End of the World As We Know It: Faith, Fatalism, and Apocalypse in America. New York: New York University Press.

Juergensmeyer, Mark (2003) Terror in the Mind of God: The Global Rise of Religious Violence (3rd edn.). Berkeley, CA: University of California Press.

Davies, William (2018) Nervous States: How Feeling Took Over the World. London: Cape.

Index

Abascal, Santiago 78, 107
Abrahamic religions 9, 32, 34, 41
Afghanistan 12–13, 22, 25, 63, 66, 94, 110
agency 62–66, 69
al-Qaeda 9, 12–13, 58, 95, 110
Amish 9, 39, 41, 84, 87, 90–92
Anglican Communion 10, 65, 92–94; Mainstream 64, 93; Mission in England 64
apocalypse 48–49, 112–116
Archbishop of Canterbury 102
artefacts 15
Atta, Mohammed 58–60
attributions 40, 48, 57, 62, 113
Attwood, Margaret 106
Australia 92–94

beliefs 3, 31–50, 84, 89; apocalyptic 112–114; and binaries 35, 38–40; core 3, 32–44, 50, 85; secondary 3, 33, 46–50; theory of 31–32
believers 39–40, 56–57, 59, 62, 70–71
Bible 11, 18–19, 32–33, 46, 102
binaries 35, 38–42, 80, 115
bin Laden, Osama 78
Bolsonaro, Jair 107
boundaries 39, 84–85
Brazil 63
Brethren *see* Plymouth Brethren
British Social Attitude Surveys 64
Bush, George W. 59

Calvin, John 63
Calvinists 63–65, 86, 92–94
causality 48, 57
change 57–58

choice 31–32, 50
Christian Europe 106–107
Church of England 63–65; of Ireland 10
church planting 92
colonialism 109
Committee for Virtue and Vice 12, 23, 39
conflict 38–44, 77–78, 85
conformity 41–44, 69–70, 83–87
conversion 16, 66; therapy 65
core beliefs 3, 32–44
courtiers 71–72

defence mechanisms 70
defensive organisation 89–92
Deobandi 13, 25
depersonalisation 57–60
Derby, John Nelson 11
differentiation 41–44, 84, 99–102
discipling 85–86
doctrine 46, 63–65

Egypt 109–110
Enlightenment 100, 103
Erdogan, Recep 78, 109
Europe 106–108

faithfulness 16
Falwell, Jerry (Sr.) 36, 71, 79
Falwell, Jerry (Jr.) 71
fight or flight 47–50
flying bishops 65
France 102, 107
function systems *see* social, systems

Gabriel 34
globalisation 100

Index 119

God 33–34, 46–47
God's Word 33–36, 38–40, 47, 50
golden age 26, 40, 107–109
Graham, Billy 12
Graham, Franklin 71

Hadith 13
Handmaid's Tale 106
Haredim 36, 39, 41–43, 46, 49, 66, 79, 87, 91–92
hijackers 58–60
Hindu 9
history 48–49, 57, 69
Holy Communion 19–20, 43, 65–66, 87, 93
Hungary 106–107

identity 39–42, 55–60, 101, 115–116
India 9, 63, 109
Industrial Revolution 64, 100
institutions 83, 116
integration 101–103
International Churches of Christ 55
interpretation 35, 44, 46–47, 50
intratextuality 19, 33
Iran 63, 109
ISIS 9, 13, 94, 110
Israel 36, 43, 63, 91

Jensen, Peter 93
Jensen, Philip 93
Jerusalem 72
jihad 12, 22, 24

Karzai, Hamid 13
Knesset 43, 49, 79

leadership 4, 77–81, 84, 106–109
Le Pen, Marine 107
letters of commendation 20, 39
LGBT 64, 107
Lipman, Dov 79–80
Lutheran Church 108

madrassahs 10, 13, 22–23
martyrdom 60
Mawdudi, Abu Ala 58, 110
McKean, Kip 85
meaning 55–60
Meloni, Giorgia 107
Middletown 86
missionaries 18–19
modernity 4, 26, 35, 89, 99–104

Modi, Narendra 9, 78, 107
Moore College 93
Moral Majority 49, 71
Moses 34, 69
movements 4, 83–84
Muncie, Indiana 86
Muslim Brotherhood 110

narrative 3, 40–41, 44, 103, 113–116
nationalism 26, 106–110
nation states 109–110
NATO 12–13
needs 41, 55–72
Netanyahu, Benjamin 50, 72, 78–80, 107
Netherlands 107
New World Order 41
Northern Alliance 12–13

obedience 39, 42, 65–66
obituaries 10, 15–16
Orban, Viktor 78, 106–107
organisation 89–95
orthodoxy 46, 63–65

Pakistan 13, 25
Pashtun 12, 22, 25
patriarchy 16–17, 19, 64, 69, 80–81, 86
Perkin, Paul 65
persecution 70, 108
personal identity 5, 55–56
Philadelphia Church of Christ 85–86
Plymouth Brethren 3, 10–12, 15–20, 33, 80, 84
populism 106–110
postmillennialism 48–49
power 103–104
premillennialism 48–49
Presbyterian 86
Prophet Mohammed 13, 25, 34, 69
prototypes 40, 77–79, 83
psychology 4–5, 31–32, 50, 70–72, 107–108
purity 60, 63–65, 87
Putin, Vladimir 102, 109

Qu'ran 12–13, 22–24, 32–34, 46
Qutb, Sayyid 58, 110

rapture 48–49
rational choice theory 31–32, 50
Reconstructionists 46

Reform 64, 93
Reformation 63–64, 100
religion 102–103, 107–108, 113–115
restorationism 26, 40, 107–109
rituals 60
Robertson, Pat 71
Roe vs. Wade 63
Roman Catholic Church 109
Russian Orthodox Church 102

Salafist 25
sanctions 23, 84
Satan 38–44
Saudi Arabia 13, 25
sects 10–12, 35, 42, 47
secularisation 99, 102
selectivity 47, 50
self: -concept 55–57; -esteem 68–72; -help 62
separation 60, 63–65, 87
sharia 12–13, 24–25, 66
Shia 22, 24
snake handling 70
social identity 39, 55–60, 62; processes 26, 77; systems 4–5, 26, 35, 77, 99–104, 110
sociology 2
sola scriptura 63
Spain 107
stereotypes 40
Sufi 22, 24
Sunnah 13
Supreme Court 63, 72
Sydney Anglicans 92–94

Taliban 3, 9–10, 12–13, 22–26, 32–33, 66, 85, 94, 110
Tamney, Joseph 85
testimonies 17
theocracy 63, 109–110
Torah 34, 39, 46, 49, 91
Trump, Donald 63, 71–72, 78, 102, 107, 109
Truth Church 86–87
truth criteria 100

Ukraine 102, 109
ultra-orthodox 36, 39, 41–43, 46, 49, 66, 78, 87, 91–92
United States 1, 11–13, 58–60, 62–63, 90
Us vs. Them 38–44, 77–78, 85

values 3, 47–48, 100, 103
victimhood 70, 108
Virtue and Vice Committee 12, 23, 39

Wade vs. Roe 72
Wahhabi 13, 25
war 58–60
Watt, David Harrington 85
West Virginia 70
Westminster Creed 86
When Prophecy Fails 70
Wilders, Geert 107
women 13, 16–17, 19, 23, 64, 69, 80–81, 86
World Council of Churches 102

For Product Safety Concerns and Information please contact our EU representative GPSR@taylorandfrancis.com
Taylor & Francis Verlag GmbH, Kaufingerstraße 24, 80331 München, Germany

www.ingramcontent.com/pod-product-compliance
Lightning Source LLC
Chambersburg PA
CBHW051754230426
43670CB00012B/2283